BRITAIN IN OLD PHOTOGRAPHS

AROUND STONY STRATFORD

A SECOND SELECTION

AUDREY LAMBERT

SUTTON PUBLISHING LIMITED

Sutton Publishing Limited
Phoenix Mill · Thrupp · Stroud
Gloucestershire · GL5 2BU

First published 1996

Cover photographs: *front*; John Thomas Webb
enjoying a mug of tea, 1929: *back*; the new
outdoor swimming pool at Fegan's Homes,
c. 1950.

British Library Cataloguing in Publication Data
A catalogue record for this book is available from the
British Library.

ISBN 0-7509-1112-3

Typeset in 10/12 Perpetua.
Typesetting and origination by
Sutton Publishing Limited.
Printed in Great Britain by
Ebenezer Baylis, Worcester.

Haymaking on the Duke of Grafton's Wakefield Estate, Potterspury, *c*. 1913. In the background are
telegraph poles on the A5 road. The building on the right was formerly the Reindeer Inn and the round
tin barn on the left was pulled down to build houses.

CONTENTS

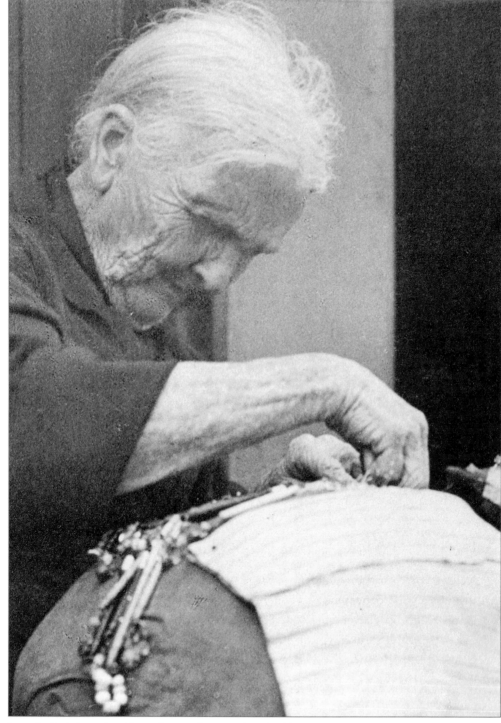

Mrs Elizabeth 'Betsy' Willett (née Daniels). A widow for fifty years, she made a living by making pillow lace and lived in Shenley Almshouses (Stafford's Cottages). She died in 1938 aged ninety and could remember the stagecoaches passing on the nearby Watling Street.

FOREWORD

Stony Stratford and its neighbourhood are lucky to have such an assiduous chronicler as Audrey Lambert. In this, her second collection of photographs from the past, she once again provides delightful glimpses of life as it used to be before so much of the area was transformed by development, and before the special qualities of village life succumbed to the motor car.

The pictures will give immense pleasure to those who enjoy spotting familiar names and places, and for those of us whose memories go back a long time, it will provide a marvellous excuse for nostalgia. I was thrilled to find the picture of the Clyno on page 68, as my mother possessed an identical car at about the same date, and I can vividly recall riding in it in the early 1930s.

The book is not just an exercise in nostalgia, however, and I hope that even those who are new to the area will find something in it for themselves. Local history adds depth to our appreciation and understanding of where we live. It can reveal much more of the detailed texture of life than more general historical studies. Though much of what is recorded here is very personal, it conveys a sense of communities where people knew each other, and were proud of their institutions, and were public-spirited in their commitment to them. Such things are worth celebrating. If at times we feel the lack of them in our own day, then it is worth recalling both the strengths and the limitations of the relatively closed communities pictured in this book, to see what we can learn from them.

When recently I had the unusual privilege of choosing a title for myself, I decided that this was a good opportunity to honour my roots. The first house I remember was Calverton House in Calverton Road, Stony Stratford. Later my family moved into Calverton Cottage in Calverton itself. I therefore took the name Baron Habgood of Calverton. Our first home is where we learn all the important lessons.

I am also glad to appear in one of the photographs in this book – but I am not saying which.

John Habgood
former Archbishop of York
1996

Building hayricks at Emerson Farm, Shenley Brook End, *c.* 1910, using a Messrs E. & H. Roberts of Deanshanger's Elevator with horse gear.

THE TOWN OF STONY STRATFORD

Heaviest of all 'notable bells' in the British Isles is Great Paul, nearly 9 ft high and 10 ft in diameter, weighing 334 cwts 2 qrs 19 lbs, seen here on the outskirts of Stony Stratford. It was taken by road from Loughborough to St Paul's Cathedral, London in 1882, a journey which took eleven days, three of which were spent in getting out of the mire at Little Brickhill.

Do you like our snowman? Clarence Road children play in the snow in the late 1950s, from left to right are; Maureen Wildman, Janet Skipper, Madeline Townsend and Kathleen Aylott. Their snowman was made on the road outside No. 84, before the advent of parked cars!   (Photograph by Audrey Waine.)

Enjoying his birthday party in 1937 is Ian Phelps – at the front in a York House school blazer – with David Ridge (on horse), Doreen Pacey and John Cowley. On the left: John Herbert (on horse), Jean Turney, Eleanor Cowley and Keith Wilyman. The older boys are; left, Ron Phelps, later captain of Stony Stratford Thursday's Football Club; right, Arnold Phelps. This picture was taken in the field at the rear of W.J. Phelps, Bakery, 119 High Street.

On the Horsefair Green with their ponies are Michael Stock on Toby and Sue Fitch (left) and her friend Cathryn Stock with Misty, c. 1969. Originally owned by the Lord of the Manor of Calverton, the Green has been a public recreation ground for 136 years. At the centre is the Baptist Church rebuilt in 1823 and the narrow three-storey house built by Thomas Williat in about 1764.

The proud owner of this tricycle in the 1940s is Lesley Shean with his older brother Ken standing behind. Their friend, John Henson, is in the background.

Beryl Walters shows off her new doll's pram in the garden of her home, 122 Wolverton Road, c. 1925.

A souvenir of their family holiday at Morecambe, c. 1924. Left to right: Jack, Bill (in blazer) and Edna Goodridge. This photo was taken in a studio, not on the beach, which was the practice before cameras were in general use.

A charming photo of four young Yates brothers from Jubilee Terrace, taken in 1902. Left to right are Wally, Will, Tom and Fred. When E. & H. Roberts, Deanshanger burnt down, Fred ran 2 miles over the fields to try and retrieve his toolbox, rather than use his new bicycle! He became a well-known cricketer and local councillor in the Wolverton Urban District Council.

In the field behind the Water Tower, at the Calverton Road and Augustus Road junction, are Mavis Huckins (left) and her sister Doris (later Mrs Sidney Capel), c. 1933. Built in 1884 by John Franklin for Stony Stratford Parish Council, the Water Tower was demolished in about 1950. Houses now cover this area.

This Cooper family portrait taken in 1899 shows John and his wife Ada (née Willett of Shenley), their daughter Florrie, holding the hoop, and Harry. John raced penny-farthing cycles from Old Stratford, straight down the hill into Stony Stratford. Hoops were a spring pastime – wooden for girls and younger children and iron ones for boys – bowled down the roads with sticks, when they were free of cars.

The Castle Orchestra was formed on 4 October 1895. Second on the left is J.W. Smith, conductor and next to him S. Sayers jnr with a three-string double bass. Centre: extreme right, John Franklin; second right, Sarah Butcher; third right, Thomas J. Tibbetts. Front: extreme right, W. Butcher. Other members include: F.W. Downing, Arthur Tibbetts, William Harris, G.W. Berry, G.F. Lever and N.H. Capell. They played at the Scala Cinema before a pianist was engaged.

Being honoured by Queen Mary in about 1949 is Nurse Elsie Wakefield, a long-time district nurse with Nurse Mary Tanner. The QIDNS on her shoulder stands for the Queen's Institute District Nurses Service. Throughout her nursing career, she was presented to three generations of the Royal Family; Queen Mary, George VI and Queen Elizabeth II. She was a keen hockey player, scored for Stony Stratford Cricket Club for some years and was a Local and County Councillor until 1974.

The 'Tuesday Club', St Mary's Parish Room, in the 1960s. Left to right: Mrs Coombs, Mrs Berry, Mrs H. Yates, Mrs Rose, Miss Green and Mr Harry Morris. Annie Knight started the club for the parish church in 1969. They had some happy meetings and outings over the years but latterly with depleted numbers, it closed before Christmas 1995.

Members of the Cadet Unit of Stony Stratford Detachment (Bucks 112) of the British Red Cross Society, 1969. Their HQ is the former Primitive Methodist Chapel in Wolverton Road. Standing, left to right: Julie Swann, ? Nicholls, Laura Youlton, Nigel Benn, Jeremy Benn, Miss Milk (Director, Youth & Juniors), Mrs Newnes (Director, Northampton Red Cross Society), -?-, -?-, -?-, -?-, Michael Ladd. Front: -?-, -?-, Judith Palmer, Julie Williams, Karen Mann, Julie Pritchard.

Red Cross 'Over 60' Club, 1982. Behind, left to right: Lotte Lucas, -?-, Mrs Bennett, ? Lawson, Julie Franklin, Mrs Hanlon (hidden), Doll Webster, Ann Roff, Edie Daniels, Ivy Robinson, Mr Wildman, Edna Wildman, Edie Smith, Rose Springall, Doll Dillow. Front: Miss Allen, Janet Williams (Red Cross Leader), Mrs Lowen, Rennie Foolkes (helper), Madge Brown, Maggie ?, Beat Aylott, Miss Manders. The 150 members raised £270 for Milton Keynes Hospital from coffee mornings selling over 1,000 cakes and buns.

In March 1963 the deeds of York House, for many years a private school, were handed over to St Giles' Youth Club. Their four-phase redevelopment scheme cost £16,000. Brothers Bill and Reg Barby explain their scale model of York House, which took them two months to complete, to Mr J.H. Irving. Looking on are Barry Wilkinson, John Welch and -?-.

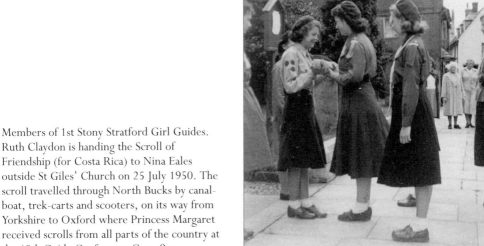

Members of 1st Stony Stratford Girl Guides. Ruth Claydon is handing the Scroll of Friendship (for Costa Rica) to Nina Eales outside St Giles' Church on 25 July 1950. The scroll travelled through North Bucks by canal-boat, trek-carts and scooters, on its way from Yorkshire to Oxford where Princess Margaret received scrolls from all parts of the country at the 40th Guide Conference Campfire.

2nd Stony Stratford Boy Scouts and Wolf Cubs with leaders and helpers, pictured on the lawn of St Mary's Vicarage, *c.* 1942, shortly after its formation by Mrs C.M. Campbell of 'Braemar', Wolverton Road. The group has since amalgamated with 1st Stony Stratford. Back row, left to right: -?-, Ray Price, Ron Robinson, Derek Hodgson, Arnold Clarke, Ian Phelps, -?-, Keith Jackman, Colin Foale, Gerald Payne. Second row: Derek Morris, Eric Stimson, Ken Ward, Ron Mackerness, Ken Eales, John Herbert, Cyril Stimson, Tony Parker, Lawrence Smith, Tony King. Centre row: David Osborne, -?-, Jack Black, Mr N.E. Chipperfield, Mrs C.M. Campbell, -?-, Evelyn Ware, Mrs Foale, Mr Cheesman, Roy Gregory, David Townsend. Second to front row: -?-, John Osborne, John Thornton, Norman Smith, John Henson, -?-, Ron Dumbleton, Ron Holbrook, Jon Garner, John Knight. Front row: -?-, Peter Garner, Arnold Smith, -?-, -?-, Peter Styles (behind), David Brown, Tony Beckett, Barry Gidman, Douglas Bates, Trevor Jackman.

(*Opposite, bottom*) A colourful charity pageant organized by members of the Women's Conservative Association in about 1936/7 taken outside their Club at the Regent Hall, St Mary's Avenue. This building is now a factory. Back row, left to right: Mrs Habgood, -?-, Miss Kitty Sibthorpe, Mrs Payne, Edna Hurst, -?-, Mrs Ceasar, -?-, -?-. Centre: Lil Downing, Mrs Eaton, Phyllis Wells, Lilian Fossey, Daphne Phillips, Joan Tompkins, Mrs Foddy (John Bull), Nora Adams, Jean Foddy, Joyce Turner, -?-, Daisy Hurst, -?-. Children, in the centre: Mary Lunn, Connie Rix, Maud Wildman (Britannia), Jean Turney, Mavis Bennett. Sitting in the front: Mrs Young, Mrs Mackerness, Mrs Gammage, -?-.

Opening a British Legion fête in the 1930s on the lawn of his home, Calverton House, is Dr A.H. Habgood from the local doctors' practice of Bull, Habgood & Lawrence. On his left is Sir Frank Markham, MP. Note the two reporters with shorthand notebooks who worked for local newspapers; on the left is Joey Allen, from the *Wolverton Express*.

A Victorian wedding, thought to be the first time a bride and groom travelled by motor car from the church in Stony Stratford. The car is a Daimler with bodywork made by Salmons of Newport Pagnell. The scene is Vicarage Road in either 1897 or 1898. Annie Franklin, the bride, was a member of the town's well-known family of builders while her bridegroom was Dick Ashley, who was then on his way to becoming a big industrialist in South Wales. The group are, left to right: Win Bailey, Amy Holland, George Franklin, Lot Bailey, Elizabeth Franklin, Miss Millward, Lewis Ashley, Richard Ashley snr, Mrs Ashley, Liz Holland (half face), Herbert Franklin, Albert Ashley (half face), the car driver, Violet Ashley (bridesmaid), Annie Franklin (bride), Dick Ashley (bridegroom), Alice Ashley (bridesmaid), Mr and Mrs John Franklin, Nell Ashley (bridesmaid), Cissie Kingston (bridesmaid), Tom Franklin, Emily Franklin (Herbert's wife), Edwin Franklin, Jessie Holland (in the background), Nellie Kingston.

A Women's Institute event, *c.* 1938. From left to right are Mrs Foddy, 7 Clarence Road (Henry VIII), Mrs Mary Rix (Catherine of Aragon) and Miss Kitty Sibthorpe, 17 Clarence Road (lady-in-waiting). Mrs Rix's husband had a butcher's shop at 78 Wolverton Road. She is now 102 years of age.

The 1st Stony Stratford Scouts, winners of Wolverton District Sports, which were held in Fegan's Homes field by kind permission of the Superintendent, Capt. E.P. Flood in 1953. Back row, left to right: Keith Brewer, David Hillyer, Verdun Parker (Rover Leader), Ken Gallop, David Phillips, Raymond Styles. Second row: Roy Skipper, Clive Andrews, Derek Church, Brian Best, David Larner, Roy Taylor. Third row, sitting: John Saunders, Graham Holdom, Brian Read, George Dicks (Group Scoutmaster), David Nash, Peter Phillips, John Roberts. Front row: Ray Holbrook, Barry Church, Frank Eglesfield, John Aylott, Ronald Hamilton, Brian Bradshaw.

Children from the market square in fancy dress to celebrate the Coronation of Queen Elizabeth II, 2 June 1953. Left to right: Michael Read, -?-, Glenis Nutt, Linda Reid, Michael Evans, Julie Evans, Richard Odell, Sue Holland.

Choirboys of St Giles' and St Mary's churches who met at the sports ground for their annual Cricket Challenge Match, Ascension Day 1961. This event ceased on the amalgamation of the two churches, now called St Mary & St Giles'. Back row, left to right: Revd H.F. Painter (St Mary's), Michael Miles, Paul Page, Martin Best, Malcolm Rose, Johann Gregory, Peter Cockerill, Rodney Henson, Roger Woodward, Revd C.L.G. Hutchings (St. Giles). Centre: Roland Daniels, Paul Hepworth, John Reynolds, Ken Dillow, Paul Martin, Eric Burgess. Front row: Michael Stock, Clive Burgess, David Meakins, Peter Eglesfield, Alan Statham, Graham Brown, Andy Canvin, Peter Chapman, Malcolm Chapman.

The open-air service held in the market square to commence the day of celebration for the Coronation of Queen Elizabeth II conducted by Revd C.L.G. Hutchings, RD (vicar of St Giles), Revd K.W. Wright (vicar of St Mary's), Revd George Higgins (Congregational) and Revd A.B. Berry (Baptist); George Webb jnr is seated at the piano. Back, left to right include: Mrs Harris, Mrs Gibbs, Les Aylott, Roger Stewart, Mrs Fielding, Eddie Cooper, Mrs Hillyer, Lewis Clark, Mr Allen, Eileen Hillyer, Joy Small, Mrs Buxton. Wearing surplices, from left: Doug Buswell, Harry Osborne, John Osborne, Arthur Webb, Tom Trasler, George Webb snr, David Townsend, Cyril Brown. From left (boys), 2nd row: Stuart Smith, -?-, Michael Sawford, John Frisby, -?-; (extreme right) -?-, Rodney Langridge, Peter Osborne, Gordon Bradshaw. Front (boys): Trevor Smith, -?-, Bill Barby, John Roberts, Oswald Tee, -?-, David Best, Tony Holland, Keith Henson, John Aylott, John Savage, Clive Bradshaw. Congregation, front right include: Miss Sylvia Clarke, Mrs Greenhall, Mrs Kingsley, Mr and Mrs H.E. Meacham.

Two of the first ladies to benefit from living in The Retreat; Mrs Ellen Meacham (née Speakes), left, wearing a cape and Mrs Jeffs, right, wearing a shawl, c. 1894. The five cottages, now four, were erected in 1892 at the sole cost of Mr Frederick William Woollard and he presented them to the town for the use of the worthy and aged poor.

John Wesley's five visits to the town included an occasion when he is reputed to have preached under the elm tree on the Market Square. The service held on 21 May 1988, which coincided with the 144th anniversary of the Silver Street Methodist Church, was also a Circuit Wesley Event.

Ladies from the Baptist Church seen here in colourful costumes but the event is not recorded. This picture was taken at the home of Mr and Mrs Ulph Woollard in Claremont Avenue, 1940–45. Back row, left to right: Mrs Wright, Mrs Nash, Mrs Taylor, Mrs Birch, Mrs Ulph Woollard, Mrs Godwin, Miss Peggy Godwin, Mrs Wilmin. Middle row: Mrs Holman, Mrs Young, Mrs Downing, Mrs Allen, Mrs Curwood (minister's wife), Mrs Stella Woollard, Miss Carden, Miss Bridgman, Mrs Brandon's mother, Mrs Calladine, Mrs Hillyer, Mrs Yates. Front row: Mrs H. Tooley, Miss Emma Harris, Mrs Harris, Miss Benson, Miss E. Elston, Mrs Reg Benbow, Mrs Williams, Mrs Birkett.

Mothers with their bonnie babies at the Welfare in 1957. Back row, left to right: Mrs Trezise Goldney, Mrs Jack Reid, ? Reid, Mrs Erridge, baby ?, -?-, Mrs Beckett, baby ?, Julie Fossey, Mrs Molly Fossey, Margaret Barden, Mrs Mary Payne, Colin Payne, Dorothy Chipperfield, Lynda Chipperfield, Mrs Rose Barden, Mrs Hepworth. From back, second row: Mrs Kath Webster, Caroline Webster, Mrs Sheila Benbow, ? Benbow, girl -?-, Mrs Nellie Neale, Annette Neale, Mrs Kit Daniels, Roland Daniels, David Gallop, Mrs Mary Gallop, Mrs Shirley Dixon, Carol Dixon, Mrs Vera Drinkwater, Keith Drinkwater, -?-, -?-, -?-, -?-, -?-. From front, second row: Mrs Doreen Longhurst, Jamie Longhurst, -?-, -?-, Mrs Barbara Taylor, ? Taylor, -?-, -?-, -?-, -?-, Mrs Connie Valentine, -?-, -?-, Mrs Betty Beeton, Robert Beeton, boy -?-, Graham Beeton, Mrs Freer, ? Freer, -?-, Nurse Elsie Wakefield. Front row: Mrs Violet Savill, Cyril Savill, Mrs Enid Stimson, ? Stimson, Mrs Ruth Berry, Julie Berry, Mrs Lily Sharp, Lynda Sharp, -?-, -?-, Miss Lines holding Stephen Willmer, Welfare Doctor holding -?-, -?-, -?-, Mrs Olive Benn holding Jeremy Benn and Mandy Webb, Louise Scrivens holding Timothy Benn, Mrs Sylvia Williams, Gregory Williams. Sitting in front: William Savill, Michael Ladd, Ian Stewart, -?-.

This row of pretty girls from the Gwendolyn Randall Dancing Troupe are performing at one of the pantomimes for St George's Church, Wolverton, c. 1948. From left to right are Valerie Parks, Yvonne Clark, Rosalie Goodman, Coral Croxall, Valerie Andrews, Pamela Judd, Ann Williams and Pat Goodman.

The tennis section of Stony Stratford Sports Club. This is the Stony Stratford 1st who played Gt. Missenden Tennis Club in 1952. Back row: Denis Chipperfield, Stan Hall, Maurice Pell, Dudley Sackett. Front row: Norman Cosford, Roy Llewellyn.

Stony Stratford Cricket Club at Ancell Sports Ground in 1936. Back row, left to right: Bert Westley (umpire), Jack Dixey, Fred Yates (chairman), Ben Cahill, Tony Barron, Harold Smith, Bill Flint, Sid Whitehead. Front row: Stan Cockerill, Les Faulkner, Bill Trevina, Tom Parks (captain), Ivan Hodgson, George Foddy.

The cricket team lined up before making an arch with cricket bats for a fellow cricketer Derek Church and his bride Ruth Peat at St Mary's Church in the late 1950s. Left to right: Anthony Pyne, John Grimsley, Barry Church, Trevor Brown, John Downing, Rodney Cleaver, Bill Bessell, Ken Jelley, Vic Tomkins, John Savage.

Stony Stratford Judo Club was formed by Verdun Parker who gained the coveted Black Belt in 1962. This is his annual competition for club members only and cups and medals were awarded according to competitors' weights. Verdun is standing behind the contestants.

The winner! John Hillyer of Stony Stratford Judo Club receiving the shield and a personal trophy from the Mayor of Bedford, Councillor David Lennox Lamb and his wife, after winning the Bedfordshire Open Championship in 1979/80.

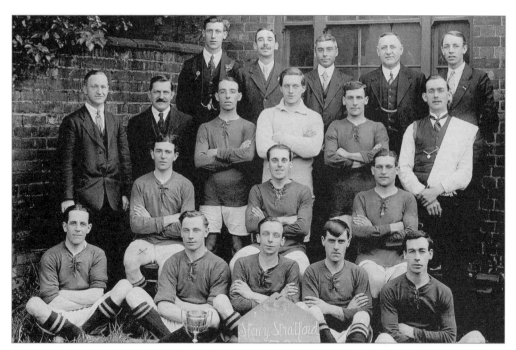

A very keen and successful team, the Stony Stratford Football Club had just won the North Bucks League in the 1919–20 season. Back row, left to right: Mr Stone, Mr Morris, Alfred Cooper, Alan Giles, Mr Davies. Second row: -?-, Mr Barley, Mr H. Morris, Percy Jelley, W. Tapp, -?-. Sitting, centre: Wally Nicholls, ? Claridge, H. Tapp. Front row: Ceilam Jelley, Mr Roberts, W. Stokes, D. Bourne, Tom Dicks.

There has been a Yates in Stony Stratford Fire Brigade since 1894. Mr Edwin Yates (centre) completed thirty-six years, retiring as Chief Officer in 1929. He was succeeded by his son, Arthur, who retired after forty years service when this photograph was taken in 1953, and his son, David (left) continued the family link. At that time, all three generations were still actively engaged in the family business of wheelwright and carpentry in Horn Lane.

Stony Stratford Football Club were runners-up in the South Midlands League, Division One during the 1948–9 season. Back row, left to right: Stan Coles (trainer), George Henson (captain), Ray Meakins, Cyril Chapman, Sam Bird, Reg Russell, Harold Russell, Ernie Richardson (chairman). Sitting: Harold Bates, Stan Russell, Lionel Exley, Ken Holbrook, Alec Smith, Dennis Lovell (secretary). Front: Michael Taylor (ball boy).

George Henson (who is also in the above photo) was Stony Stratford's most famous professional footballer from 1929 to 1939. He had spells with five different teams. His greatest personal achievements were whilst playing for Bradford Park Avenue, scoring 6 goals in a 7–1 victory against Blackburn Rovers on 29 January 1938 in a Football League, Division Two match. He was the Top Scorer in Div. II in the 1937/8 season with twenty-seven goals to his credit – plus six more in Cup Competitions. Unfortunately the Second World War finished his professional football career. Thereafter, he played for Bedford Town and Stony Stratford and retired in 1951.

Posing on the edge of the croquet lawn and with the school in the background, are members of the combined fifth and sixth forms of York House School, *c.* 1932. Back row, left to right: Eleanor Phipps, Kathleen Gardner, Eileen Higgs, *Dora Mackerness, *Kathleen Fairburn, *Mary 'Biddy' Gerrard, Constance Saunders, Joan Rogers. Centre: *Vera Higgs, Louise Moodie, Miss Dorothy Slade. Front: *Maisie Holland, Molly Coker, Beatrice Cowley. (* = sixth formers.)

Having fun in the Percussion Band at York House School, *c.* 1933. Top: Conductor, name unknown. Back, left to right: Barry Toms, James Montgomery, -?-, Barbara Waymark, David Leigh's sister, Margaret Cowley, John Haseldine, -?-, Leslie White, David Leigh. Centre: Jean Andrews, Leslie White's sister. Front: Barbara Singleton, Doreen Pacey, Geoff Waymark, -?-, Keith Wilyman.

'Here's our guy and we're all ready for Guy Fawkes Night', *c.* 1948. This event was much enjoyed at Fegan's Homes when potatoes were cooked in the fire and everyone had a mug of cocoa. The boy on the right, Jimmy Harris, when retrieving his tennis ball from the roof gutters, leaned over too far and survived a fall of 40 feet to the tarmac below with no broken bones!

The opening of the new outdoor swimming pool at Fegan's Homes, *c.* 1950. It was the first pool of its kind in the area and district schools were allowed to use it. The boys are making an 'F' for Fegan – Mr J.W.C. Fegan being the founder.

Under the archway entrance to St Anthony's Franciscan School are Father Terence, headmaster and on the right, Canon C.H.J. Cavell-Northam, vicar of St Mary & St Giles, *c.* 1968. This Roman Catholic school closed in 1972.

St Giles Church of England Boys School, near the White Swan, High Street, *c.* 1931. This is Class 7, Mr W. Toms', the headmaster's, class. Back row, left to right: Ray Downing, Bill Crossman, Wallace Underwood, Harry Atkins, Doug Dunkley, Mr W. Toms (headmaster), Ted Swain, Bob Jackson, Bert Larner, Stan Whitlock, Wilf Sims. Middle row: Leslie Lovesy, Archie Caudle, Willie Alderman, Cecil Bailey, Philip Wilmin, Sid Davis. Front row: Aubrey Bishop, Fred Brown, Percy Pratt, Frank Sharman, Frank Wright. Mr 'Billy' Toms started his teaching career aged fourteen in 1903, as a pupil teacher; he retired forty-eight years later in 1951.

St Mary's Church School, built in 1873, is now the Plough Inn. The headmistress is Miss Lydia Hayes; teacher Miss Elsie Butcher (later Mrs Arthur Tyrell); pupil teacher Miss Florence Amelia Cooper (later Mrs Herbert Waine). Back row, left to right: *Winnie Davis, Ada Holman, *Nellie Clark, Jessie Smith, *Alice Tuckwell, May Beard, *Florrie Jones, Ruth Thompson, *Lottie Cox, Florence Cooper. Centre row: Miss Lydia Hayes, Miss Elsie Butcher, *Alice Percy, Ethel Baker, Winnie Gillard, *Mabel Foster, Laura Gallop, Annie Biddle, Lavinia Aldridge, Lizzie Aldridge, Eva Nicholls, Nellie Brown. Front row: -?-, Mabel Bull, *Irene Longstaff, Annie Baker, Lizzie Wise, Ethel Smith, Lily Stevens, Alice Bennett, Louie Swann. (* indicates girls from a home. They were brought up by various families in the town with their own children.)

Russell Street School, *c.* 1925. This Council School was opened in 1907 as a mixed establishment to take 200 pupils. Back row, left to right: Bill Chapman, Cyril Conner, -?-, -?-, Fred Atkins, Vic Smith, Cecil Coles, Vic Ratcliffe, Fred Stanton, ? Clarke. Centre row: Sam Neale, Marion Blackburn, Violet Buswell, Doris Gayton, Maggie Lovell, Rita White, -?-, Hubert Bawden, Walter Toombs, -?-. Front row: Maggie Chapman, Vera Day, Eva Sayers, -?-, May Hamilton, Martha Manders, Irene Clarke, Lil Fisher, Lil Farmer, Winnie Puryer.

A picture of a smiling Mrs Gladys Cropper, for many years head of the Nursery School – formerly Miss Holland of Vicarage Road – with children and helpers in about 1946. Back row: Mavis Brown, Mrs Violet Wilkes, Olive Saving. Standing: Mavis Dearn, Philip Clewitt, Jill Henson, Malcolm Swann, George Mills, Yvonne Fensom, Joan Butcher, Major Howe. Sitting: Valerie Carpenter, Roger Benn, Denise Duggan, Christopher Flint, Mrs Gladys Cropper, Trevor Read, Michael Dicks, Susan Baker, Peter Quinn. Front row: Alan Richardson, Tony Holland, Hazel Wilkes, Robert Bruce, Gwen Foote, Harold Bailey, Christine Ley.

A class from the Stony Stratford Primary School, Russell Street, *c*. 1947. Back row, left to right: Margaret Wrightson, Ann Underhill, Edna Colborne, -?-, Claire Lawrence, Ann Barley, Mary Jackman, Jennifer Smith, Ann Mitchell, Yvone Mackerness, Beatrice Betts, Michael Roberts, Michael Sawford, Pat Cook. Standing alone: Anne Rowledge. Middle row: -?-, Jean Cannings, Roy Green, Sylvia Chapman, Ian James, Barbara Dickens, Joan Young, John Andrews, Ronald Best, Mrs Hamilton (teacher), Linda Barley, David Weatherhead, Nancy Bolton, Dorothy Brown, Clive Bradshaw, Alan Clements, Elizabeth Richardson, Rodney Whitehead. Front row: Bernice Swann, Timothy Flint, Keith Henson, Ronald Hamilton, Brian Andrews, Rodney Cleaver, John Robinson, Colin Wrightson, Roy Trimmer, Tony Farmer, Ronald Jones, Gordon Sargent, Bernard Foote, Brendan Daniels.

Photographed with Russell Street houses in the background is a class from the Primary School with their supply teacher in 1957/8. Back row, left to right: Stephen Kenny, Michael Read, -?-, John Dolling, Graham Hutchinson, Chris Willis, John Rothwell, Michael Evans, Philip Keeling, Graham Battison, Reggie Booth. Centre row: Cyril Fletcher, Desmond Smythe, Brian Canvin, Richard Odell, Roger Perkis, -?-, John Waite, Derek Daniels, Roger Jackson, Louis Chinnery, Roy Baxter. Sitting: Margaret King, Marilyn Eaton, Dorothy Holland, Linda Westley, Ellen Beachey (teacher), -?-, Vicky Smith, Susan Neil, Lesley Johnson, -?-, Evelyn Richardson.

Class 10 of the Stony Stratford Primary School with their teacher, Miss Peach, in 1966. Top row: Jonathan Gillis, Richard England, Benjamin Nazaroo, Trevor Rush, Raymond Young, Nigel Phillips. Second row: Steven Galuszka, John Savage, Michael Whetstone, Robert Cable, Christopher Daniels, David Jones, Martin Frere, Anthony Bungay, -?-, David -?-. Third row: Robert Beeton, Neville Barr, Trevor Tearle, David Partridge, Glynis Hull, Gillian Harris, Elizabeth Holland, Miss Peach. Front row: Cathryn Stock, Mandy Funke, Yvonne Elsey, Ingrid Schuler, Ann Lawrence, Janice Forman, Kathleen Walker, Christine Barfoot, Carol Levitt.

Playing shops at Stony Stratford Primary School, *c.* 1949. Standing, left to right: Roger Dunckley, Rodney Tearle, Pat Bessell, Colin Bricknall, George Bonsell, Joy Pitkin, John Franklin, David Carter, Margaret Crouch, Chris Barrett, Michael Webb, Christine Wrightson. Sitting: Leslie Wootton, Neil Smith, Sylvia Green, Margaret Ley, Hayden Shirley, Brenda Cox, John Watts. The teacher's name is unknown.

Stony Stratford Senior School Girls PE Group photographed in June 1941 in the field behind St Giles Vicarage; the house is now demolished. Back row, left to right: Celia Bishop, Eileen Tapp, Betty Stephenson, Beryl -?-, Cynthia Clark, Phyllis Johnson, -?-. Centre row: Audrey Pearce, -?-, -?-, Betty Colton, -?-, May Jarvis, Vera Fossey, Betty Clarke, Peggy Haycock. Front row: Winnie Martin, -?-, -?-, Betty Webb, Alice Bull, -?-, Pat Cook, Jean Taylor. Those represented by a question mark may have been evacuees.

Stony Stratford Secondary Modern School in 1950. Back row, left to right: John Eales, Roger Tapp, Fred Bartholomew, Brian Canavan, Colin Gledhill, -?-, Brian Taylor, Donald Dumbleton. Second row: Margaret Mills, Janet Stones, Pauline Munday, Joyce Folwell, Miss Ada Hadley (teacher), Margaret Illing, Janet Styles, Madeline Fisher, -?-. Sitting: John Gilbert, Ian Smyth, Albert Jones, Gill Farmer, Ruth Peat, Lucy Clark, Brenda Capel, Brian Best, Peter Dimmock, Ken Savage. Front: John Giles, Eric Worth, Brian Duggan, Alan Goodridge. (All those sitting, John, Ian, Albert and Peter, were from Fegan's Homes).

The cookery class of Stony Stratford Senior School, 1945. All members had to make their own caps and aprons. Back row, left to right: Diana Eglesfield, Thelma Robinson, Ann Marks, Betty Shurmer, Joyce Colton, Ann ?, Barbara Downing, Kathleen Wrighton, Doreen Westley, Sylvia Ward, Janet Lampitt. Front row: Kathleen Cannings, Ruth Claydon, Nina Eales, Peggy Hanwell, Margaret Nicholls, Mrs Holton (teacher), Joy Aylott, Margaret Sinfield, Elizabeth Smallman, Margaret Slaymaker, Pamela Wheeler.

Photographed at the back of his home at 16 Queen Street is Doug Martin, seen here in about 1932, when working for Calladine & Son, boot and shoemakers, who had their premises at 38 High Street (now a Red Cross Charity shop). His job was to deliver both new and repaired shoes to the customers on his trade cycle.

Nimrod and Alice Benbow with sons Reg (left) and Stan (right) at 40 High Street. Nimrod Benbow came from Winslow in 1894 to take over Shephard's Bakers at this address – now Arthur Coyston, shoe repairer. In 1908, he moved to 2 High Street, formerly Mr Henry Perrin's harnessmaker's shop. He transformed it into a bakery and tea rooms. When Nimrod died in 1943, his two sons took over the business.

Stanley (left) and Reginald Benbow, kneading dough at 2 High Street. Both bread and confectionery have been made and delivered over the years. Stan travelled to Wicken and Deanshanger and later included Nash, Calverton and Beachampton in his rounds. Reg made deliveries around the town of Stony Stratford and also Shenley. After the sudden death of Stan, the bakery closed in January 1970, which brought to an end seventy-five years of Benbows Bakery.

Local pet shop owner, Cyril Wain, pictured on his retirement in November 1976, after thirty-one years in the business which he purchased from his former employer, T.G. Knight, Corn & Pet Food Merchants, 86 High Street – now the Fur & Purr Pet Shop. When twelve years old his first job, at Hall & White, the grocers at 9 High Street, was to roast the coffee beans, which sent the aroma out into the street.

Taking a well-earned 'rest' before installing the toilets in a Bletchley school are employees of Betts & Son in 1961. Back row, left to right: Tom Meakins, George James, Richard Onan. Front row: Trevor Cook, Jim Pack, Ron Hockley.

The Cowley family pictured in 1897, probably at 16 Market Square. Back row, left to right: George, Jessie, Frank, Florence Rolfe, Arthur, Harry, Ethel, Hugh. Sitting: Daniel Stears Cowley and wife Harriet (née Rolfe), daughter of George Rolfe, baker, 119 High Street, (later Phelps). Front row: Dorothy, Alan, Miriam. Daniel was the innkeeper of Bull Hotel, then a baker at 16 Market Square. His son, Hugh, continued this business, in turn followed by his son Arthur; he retired in 1991 and the bakery closed. Dorothy married Percy Phillpotts of Cox & Robinson Ltd. Miriam married Robin Rogers, a farmer from Chackmore.

During the Second World War Arthur Cowley's horse, Taffy, finds the BUK Bin outside Water Tower, Calverton Road, and has some tasty bits to eat! Bucks United Kitchens collected household food scraps and sold them to feed poultry, pigs and other livestock.

Proudly wearing his London Police uniform is George Rolfe, whose father had a bakery at 119 High Street; this is now a guest house called 'Fegan's View'. His sister Harriet married Daniel Cowley, another baker at 16 Market Square, who was a cricketer for Bucks County.

Police Inspector George Rolfe again, 21 May 1914. This huge inspector rushed forward to claim his prize, and as he carried Mrs Emmeline Pankhurst (née Goulden) bodily past a group of waiting reporters, she called out, 'Arrested at the gates of the Palace. Tell the King!'

Shown here in his dispensary, wearing his white pharmacist's coat and using his pestle and mortar, is Peter Phillpotts, a past owner of Cox & Robinson Ltd, Chemists & Druggists, 75 High Street – now Stratford Arcade. He served on many Health Committees and was appointed a Fellow of the Pharmaceutical Society of Great Britain.

Arriving in the town in 1928, Amy 'Bidge' Francis and her husband Bob took over the shop Sedgley's, 27 High Street, when her father William Sedgley became ill. They sold grocery at one end and greengrocery at the other. She continued to run the shop for five years after the death of her husband and retired in 1967.

The Meadows family captured on their tennis court behind their Draper, Milliner & Gents' Outfitter's shop, London House, 3 High Street, *c.* 1921. Back row, left to right: Ernest Gordon, Walter William Meadows, his wife Florence Mary Smith of Bicester and William Walter. Front row: Stanley and Dorothy. Walter came from his previous shop in Buckingham to the town. Ernest continued in business after the death of his father from 1926 to the 1950s when it closed.

The last carrier in the area, Teddy (Edwin) Ratcliffe from Potterspury. He could not read or write and carried many messages in his head, travelling by donkey and cart. After the donkey died in York Road, the Stony Stratford tradesmen paid for this hand-truck to be made by Edwin 'Ted' Yates. Teddy retired just after the Second World War.

Succeeding his father James Odell in the ironmongery business (Odell & Co. Ltd), Lionel (or LEO, as he signed his name) is photographed by Buttram in 1902 in his normal business dress. He delivered household, garden and ironmongery goods to surrounding villages by horse and covered wagon. The business still flourishes under the directorship of two of his grandsons, Richard and David Odell.

A delightful photograph taken in 1909 of the twin sons of Lionel Odell, Ronald (left) and Lionel Odell aged three years.

PAST MEMORIES

The fourth and last Watts to be Squire of Hanslope, the much respected Edward Hanslope Watts and his wife Sophia Edith (née Selby-Lowndes of Bletchley) were walking home, one behind the other as was their custom, from morning service at St James' Church on Sunday 21st July 1912. Suddenly a gunshot killed the Squire outright and Mrs Watts had a narrow escape. The coachman, George Green, found the body of William Farrow, the Squire's head gamekeeper and murderer, lying on a nearby track.
Interring her husband in a distant corner of the churchyard, Mrs Farrow unwisely had a stone erected on his grave bearing the inexplicable words: 'Waiting till all shall be revealed.' Pictured here is the scene of the murder, showing the main entrance to Hanslope Park, 20 yards ahead.

Enjoying a mug of tea from his teacan is John Thomas Webb, sitting by a stook in one of his cornfields and taking a welcome break from work in the harvest field on 19 September 1929. He farmed Long Street Farm, Hanslope – opposite the Globe Inn – from 1914 until 1934.

Hay harvest at Long Street Farm, Hanslope, *c.* 1930. Frank Webb is the lad on the right of the photograph.

Near Hanslope, *c.* 1940. This happy bunch of girls have been gleaning (picking up the corn left after harvesting) to feed to their poultry at home as a supplement to their food during the Second World War.

Butchers Oak in Bloggs Lawn, Hanslope, which died in about 1800. It is said that when sheep stealing was prevalent, rustlers used to skin and dress the carcases inside the hollow shell. It eventually blew down and was burnt by children from the Fresh Air Children's Fund who were sent to the country for a holiday from London in 1940. The tree was thought to be about 400 to 450 years old.

A sixth bell was erected with a donation by Stansfield Nicholson in memory of his late father Revd M.A. Nicholson MA, who was vicar at Hanslope for forty-one years. The parishioners paid for the third bell to be re-cast in 1906. Back row, on the step, left to right: Joe Kerridge, Mr Yorke the sexton. Front row, left to right: four men from the bell foundry, Squire Watts, Squire Watts' daughter, Irene, Tommy Courtman, Revd William Jardine Harkness and Mrs Harkness, Miss M. Neal, Mr Robbins, Stansfield Nicholson, Percy Evans, Swanny Gregory, the Curate.

The Hanslope band of bellringers who attended the first AGM of the Oxford Diocesan Guild of Church Bellringers, North Bucks Branch, at Newton Longville on 3 June 1905. Back row, left to right: Jack Smith, Tom Evans, Stansfield Nicholson, Teddy Nichols, Harry Warner. Front row: Jessy Kingston, Edgar Eakins, Tommy Nichols, Reg Kingston.

Senior citizens outside the Cock Inn, Hanslope in 1929. Back row, left to right, includes: J. Warren, T. Eakins, C. Webb, W. Bull, G. Herbert. Middle row: J. Chilton, J. Neal, W. Basketfield, J. Gregory, J. Soanes, G. Gostelow, F. Cook. Front row includes: J. Nichols, W. Everitt, J. Gregory, J. Geary, W. Mills, F. Hillyer.

Hanslope village football team, *c.* 1920. Back row, left to right: E. Evans, H. Brownsell, G. Chilton. Centre row: P. Rainbow, ? Clark, C. Evans. Front row: F. Herbert, A. Chilton, M. Smith, H. Cook, A. Clark.

Example of a detached 'one up and one down' house in Forest Road, Hanslope, *c.* 1920. Mr and Mrs Jim Stones are standing in the doorway.

Looking at the Machine Gun Corps Book of Remembrance are Mr Bob Garratt and Mrs Muriel Ditum with Mr Selby Davey, right, in the background. It took Bob and Muriel many hours to research War Office records and write the list of 62,049 machine gunners killed in the Great War from 1915 when MGC was formed. Dedicated in September 1969, the book is now in St Wulfram's Church, Grantham where the regimental colours are laid up.

Castlethorpe Junior School in 1937. Back row, left to right: L. Ward, H. Jordon, L. White, W. Scripps, ? Drake, J. Herbert, N. West. Second row: M. Butcher, N. Meacham, -?-, ? Fountaine, P. Ray, P. West, B. Gray, P. Markham, J. Stones. Third row: J. West, I. Atkins, J. Butcher, P. Baxter, J. Lambert, J. Hall, J. Britten. Fourth row: -?-, J. Gray, A. Lambert, B. Pittam, -?-, -?-, L. Hart, J. West, V. Clarke, L. Scripps. Front row: A. Collyer, ? Fountaine, K. Carpenter, P. Britten, -?-.

Dancing round their maypole on May Day are children from Castlethrope School in 1952. From left to right: Christine Ward, Carole Bavington, Josie Lane, Dorothy Belton, Maureen Collyer, Shelagh Meachem, unknown boy, Maureen Synnott, Susie Robinson (half hidden), Carole Keeves, Peter Thomas. Front: Carol Stevens, Anne Gray, Amy Booth. Steadying maypole: standing, John Cooper, sitting, -?-, Stuart Lane.

Castlethorpe Football Club, 'The Fresians', *c.* 1950/5. Their president Mr Billy Markham being a farmer, the club were named after his pedigree herd of cattle. They were the proud winners of the Buckingham Shield and the Division Two North Bucks League Cup. Back row, left to right: Jimmy Mills, Reg West, Paddy Mullins, Alfie Collyer, Les Ward, Derick Chilton, Jack Baxter, Bob Weston, Les Brownsell, Maurice Weston. Centre row: John Gray, Mick Parris, Stan Brownsell, Fred Lane, Joe Russell, of Hartwell (goalie), Vic Old, Jack Wilson, Ron Bates, Lol Hart, behind, Frank Freeman (trainer), Cliff Markham, behind, Bert Tapp, Bill White. Front row: George White, Manny Crick, Desmond Chilton, Francis Hill, Mr Billy Markham (President), Bert Garratt, Viv Old, Ronnie Sainsbury.

Ben Sawbridge, postmaster, with his wife Nancy and postwoman Mrs Joan Marks in 1980. Mrs Marks had done her round in Castlethorpe, on foot, for twenty years. The postmaster's day started with sorting letters before 7 a.m. then delivering the post and finishing the accounts after 6 p.m. To help the elderly, he collected their empty pill and medicine bottles every Monday in a big wicker basket, taking them to the doctor in the next village (Hanslope), who filled them up; he returned them on the Tuesday.

The results of a disastrous fire on 9 March 1908 which destroyed the thatched cottages of Mrs Course and Harry Blunt in Grafton Regis.

These picturesque cottages, seen here in about 1910, were on the main road to Northampton at Grafton Regis but sadly were demolished to widen the road. The White Hart public house can be seen in the distance on the right.

Two decorated prams in the school playground at Yardley Gobion to celebrate the Coronation of George VI on 12 May 1937. Left to right: Yvonne Dickens (in pram), Rose Dickens, Violet Rush, Fred Horton (bandsman), Harry Kightley, Elsie Kightley, Barbara Rush (in pram).

Yardley Gobion Britannia Brass Band playing in the old recreation ground on Coronation day, 12 May 1937. The conductor Joe Horton had four sons, one brother and one son-in-law in this band. In the background is the Coffee Pot on the left and Highcroft House in the centre. Back row, left to right: Sid Carter, Joe Horton (conductor), Jack Key. Centre row: Leslie Dickens (boy), Ern Dickens, Gerry Horton, Fred Horton, George Horton, Freddie Durrant, Mrs Barker. Front row: Albert Horton, Alfie Horton.

This peaceful scene in Moorend, Yardley Gobion, seen here in the 1920s, is somewhat altered today. Although the house is still there, the road has been widened, the well is covered and the windlass has gone, as has the tree on the left.

Yardley Gobion Football Club, winners of the North Bucks and District League and the Bowyers Shield in 1934–5, the first time this trophy was put up for competition. There were three sets of brothers in the team and they played Cranfield in the final in the Red Bridge Field, Bradwell. Back row, left to right: Graham Church (manager), George Glenn, George Horton (goalie), Sid Ratledge, Toby Webb (trainer). Centre row: Alf Horton, Julian Pittam, Joe Swain. Front row: Tom Kightley, John Marshall, Bill Glenn, Dick Smith, Fred Kightley.

Pink Day, Potterspury, 1920. This group is standing outside the Anchor Inn. Before the National Health Service, admission to Northampton General Hospital was by 'letter' only. This system was regulated by the number of 'letters' given to the villages in proportion to how much money they raised on Pink Day which was held each year.

Potterspury Excelsior Band, 1953. A marching band, they were reformed after a two year lapse in 1952, but were disbanded in 1961. Note the Village Hall behind them has a letter box and is No. 43 in Church End. The whole village was numbered after the Second World War. Back row, left to right: Bill Atkins, Bob Webster, Jim Bumby, John Chambers, Mr Wheeler, Tony Wootton, Sid Carter, Walt Kightley, Edgar Johnson. Boys: Les Pittam, Dennis Webster. Seated: Gary Roberts, John Smith (blacksmith), Fred Atkins, Mr Parkinson, Reg Atkins, -?-, Frank Atkins, Doug Holloway, Richard Birchall.

'The Pig on the Wall' with Syd Holloway and Jim Baseley as Old Father Time leading the village band in the Potterspury Coronation Day Parade, 2 June 1953. This custom comes from the old saying: 'The Pig got on the wall in "Pury" to watch the band go by!'

Potterspury Water and Steam Mill in the
1930s. The mill was rebuilt after a fire in the
1850s. When the dam was full, the mill only
worked for one hour and then reverted to
steam to drive the millstones. It was a four-
stone mill on Pury Brook, one of the largest
tributaries of the River Ouse and was used
until 1951. Perrin's sold their milling business
to Francis Coales & Sons, Newport Pagnell and
the mill was later converted into three houses.
(Photograph by Ken Holloway.)

There were at least three generations of the Smith family who were blacksmiths in Potterspury. They lived
nearby in the extreme left of the four cottages that made up Blacksmiths Row. Alan John Smith, a
bachelor, is shoeing a horse watched by his father, Sid Smith, in the 1930s. The man holding the horse is
unknown. The business closed when John retired.

A Potterspury School group, *c.* 1952/3. Back row, left to right: Ronald Henson, Tony Wootton, John Williams, Philip Tustain, John Kingston, Daphne Tapp, -?-, Janet Edwards, Doreen Williams. Front row, teachers: Mrs Jones, Mr Martin Jones, Mr Graham Ford, Mrs Ford, Miss Jeffs.

Three little girls from school are we! Olive, Thelma and (seated) Alfreda Webster from Potterspury, *c.* 1932.

A new treble bell bearing the names of the vicar, the Revd Rees Gwerfyl Richards, and churchwardens, Mrs M.C. Holt and Mr J.K. Soper, was added to the peal at St Nicholas, Potterspury in 1951. The other five bells were renovated and repaired by Taylors of Loughborough. The bellhanger was Horace Myatt and John Smith, the blacksmith, also assisted with the work. The third bell is pre-Reformation, made by Thos. Harries in 1479/8, and weighing in at 17 cwt.

The Potterspury Rose Queen, c. 1938. Back row, left to right: Lily Webster, Kath Henson, Joyce Hughes (Rose Queen), Winn Russell, Pat Dunkley. Front row: Syd Tapp, Pete Meakins, Phyllis Barby, Rose Barby, Gillian Tapp, Maureen Russell, Doug Holloway.

In the Recession of the late 1920s and early 1930s the Potterspury Rural District Council set men to rebuild Watling Street. This included changing the straight crossroads to a staggered road junction. Men out of work had to meet at the Anchor Inn, Potterspury, and accept any job that was offered or their dole money was withdrawn. The Anchor Inn and all the houses on the left have now been demolished.

Jimmy Holman of Cosgrove in an early hand-propelled invalid carriage in 1939. This was later converted by his family to a motorized vehicle.

Outside the Barley Mow Inn with its oil lamp on the wall is Cosgrove football team, *c.* 1923. Back row, left to right: Harry Keach, George Ray, Harry Johnson, Bert Tack, Alan Cadd (goalie), -?-, Tommy Dicks, Mark Beasley snr, Mark Beasley jnr. Centre: Bill Castle, Bob Brown, Harry (Albert) Nichols. Front: Charlie 'Wag' Eglesfield, George Jelley, Malcolm Jelley, Tom Castle, Stan Lord.

Cosgrove Football Club, winners of the Junior Buckingham Charity Cup in 1953–4. Back row, left to right: Cyril Mallows, Les Reynolds, Howard Smith, Robin Neale (goalie), Les Lyman, John Shervington, John Loughrey, Bob Jones (secretary and linesman). Front row: Keith Davis, David Lyman, Albert Rickaby, Capt. P.Y. Atkinson, Joe Hefford, Phil Tustain, Roy Rock.

A fête in May 1945 to raise money for the rebuilding of the old village hall in Cosgrove was opened by Queen Geraldine of Albania, the beautiful young Hungarian who married King Zog. The six little children are dressed as bride and groom, and attendants. Robin Winterbottom presented a bouquet of dark red carnations bound with taffeta bows of black and red – the Albanian colours. Left to right: Lady-in-waiting, Mrs Penelope Winterbottom, Queen Geraldine, a Princess. Children: Sylvia Wickham, Brenda Goodridge, Pat Bushell, Pauline Pollard, Robin Winterbottom, Frances, daughter of Mr and Mrs Charles Sweeney.

Garden staff at Cosgrove Hall, c. 1934, standing by the wheel which pumped water up from the well in the cemetery. It had two handles and needed one person each side to pump water into the tank on the left. Left to right: Jim Lambert, garden boy, Ernest Lambert, gardener, George Hooton, Alf Whitaker, gardener, Mr G.H. Winterbottom (owner), -?-.

In a heat wave in May 1947, Land Girl Olive Williams is busy sheep-shearing and just putting the finishing touches to this sheep's 'summer undies'. Farmer George Ruff of Rectory Farm, Cosgrove, looks on approvingly.

The Washing Machine from Reg Whiting's Gravel Pits, Cosgrove, c. 1936, showing the tubs pulled by horses for fetching and distributing washed gravel and sand. This was before the days of Dowsetts who supplied materials for the building of the M1 – completed in 1960 – which emptied these pits of gravel.

The towpath, Old Stratford sluice and humpback bridge, which connects Wolverton Mill meadows to the Old Stratford side and the old Lime Kiln Field. The Grand Junction Canal built the Buckingham Arm branch from Cosgrove to run to the busy turnpike road in Old Stratford in 1800. This section was 1 mile, 2.38 furlongs long. Level 14 ft beam.

The bellringers pictured in the alcove of the ringing chamber in SS Peter and Paul's church, Cosgrove, c. 1957. Note the peephole at the back for use at weddings to observe when to stop ringing on the bride's arrival and when to resume as the happy couple returned down the aisle. Back row, left to right: Gwen Barnes, Jimmy Pack, Billy Pack, John Martin, Roger Pollard, Bridget Cummings, Tony Hefford, Jim Lambert, Keith Stubbs, Roger Kightley (holding bellrope). Front row: Ian Lambert, Ted Lambert, Michael Chown.

John Higgins of Cosgrove in his motor car with his two daughters Dorothy ('Doll') in the front and Joan in the back with her dog Spot. The car is a Clyno, registration number UK 351, made at Wolverhampton in 1925. It was purchased second-hand in 1929 for £50. It rotted away in the Second World War and Mr Higgins sold it for scrap for £2.

These two smart little lads wearing knee breeches are brothers William (left) and Herbert Webb, sons of Harry and Annie Webb of Deanshangar. Their portrait was taken by F.G. Smith, in September 1898, who had premises on the High Street, Stony Stratford.

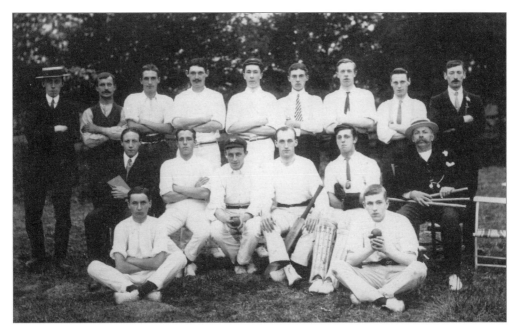

Deanshanger Ironworks Cricket Club, *c.* 1907. The club retained 'Ironworks' in its title until the E. & H. Roberts works closed in 1926. Standing, left to right: Bill Collett (secretary), Freddie Tapp, Walt Cattell, Atkins from Wicken, Vic Hyde, Jim Foddy, William Webb, Bill King, W.J. Atkinson. Sitting centre: George Hawkins (with score book), Charlie Tolley, Fred Yates, R.D. Carslake (captain), Fred King, Alf Church (manager and coach). Front: Ted Church, Eb (Ebenezer) Henson.

Deanshanger Football Club on the Buckingham Town ground, *c.* 1950. Back row, left to right: Jack Williams, Ken Sheldon, Bert Neale, Ray Janaway, Les Roberts, Harry Jones. Front row: Benny Bull, Taffy Maycock, Cyril Nicholls, Den Church, Peter Hillyer. Ball boy: Martyn Maycock.

Deanshangar School, *c.* 1923. The latticed windows behind are worthy of note. This photograph was taken on the Green near the Duke's Head public house, which is now closed. Back row, left to right: Wallace Smith, Muriel Burrows, May Foddy, Lily Greaves, Aggie Barby, Lilian Mackerness, Jim Read, Ern Johnson. In front of the school door: Ray Wilmin. Centre row: Fred Stretton, Jim Trimmings, George Johnson, Sid 'Polly' Perkins, -?-, George Church, Gerald Tapp, George Webb, ? Knibbs, Percy Drinkwater, Bill King, Reg Wyatt, Bob Price, Charlie Hall, Jack Dumbleton. Sitting: Cecil Barrett, Sid Tapp, Marjorie Burrows, Doris Bailey, Blanche Roberts, Beatrice Stretton, May Barby, Dora Bailey, Rose Tolley, Phyllis Roberts, Winnie Drinkwater, Dora Stretton, Olive Smith.

Passenham Parochial Church school, Deanshanger, *c.* 1932. This school was the winner of the South Northants Schools Championship Shield and was awarded Individual and Team Cups. Back row, left to right: Cyril Nicholls, Cyril Toombs, Wilfred Ridgeway, William Henson, Dennis Church, Albert Andrews, Lionel Longland, Reg Tite, Les Grant, Les Roberts. Centre row: Sylvia Rosson, Tom Tompkins, Alice Tompkins, Nina Robinson, Daisy Cooper, Edna Trimmings, Francis Nicholls, Gladys Price, John A. Taylor-Brown (headmaster). Front row: Phyllis Harris, Elsie Wootton, Sheila Tapp, Eileen Ridgeway, Phyllis Tite, Evelyn Neal, Olive Wootton, Yvonne Robinson, Louisa Andrews.

The results of a favourite Sunday afternoon walk from Deanshanger to Whittlebury Woods to go 'bluebelling', *c.* 1939. Now sadly the picking of these wild flowers is illegal. Back row, left to right: Ernest Tite, Phyllis Tite, Herbert Webb, Olive Webb. Centre row: Mary Simmonds. Front row: Edith Bazeley with Diane Bazeley, Rose Tite, Margaret Webb, Mary Webb.

A section of the 180 scholars and staff from Deanshanger School at their Christmas tea in the school canteen on Wednesday 20 December 1950. It was the first occasion that the scholars were able to partake of this festive tea at one sitting. The staff and friends are standing at the back. The scholars raised the money for the tea by means of an organized jumble sale. Back, left to right: Mrs Carslake, Mrs Taylor-Brown, Mr J. Taylor-Brown (headmaster), Miss Collins (teacher), Charles Pascoe (teacher), Mrs Grant (cook), Mr Conners (teacher). Front table, from back to front: Susan McNeill, Susan Webb, Kay Brazier, Douglas Knibbs, Carol Green, -?-, Theo Hall, Keith Colton, Howard Brewer, Shaun King. Second table, facing camera, from back: June Russell, Miss Hurst, Denis Nicholls, Brian Robinson, Joan Dumbleton, Ronald Easteal, Peggy Whitehead, Chris Case, Dorothy Blacknell, Jane Smith, Pamela Phillips, Barbara Sapwell. The boy to the right at the front is unknown. Others in group behind include: Mrs Barby, Maurice 'Mossy' Brown, Alan Darby, Richard Henson, Vic Rogers and Roland Barby.

The landlord, George Brazier, and a group attending the Darts Team Supper, pictured outside the Fox and Hounds Inn in the 1950s. Back, left to right: George Ridgeway, Arnold Wiley, Keith Brewer, Eric Darby (behind in doorway), Fred Whitehead, Ernie Hall, George Brazier (landlord, in doorway), Charlie Tolley, Charlie Hall, Archie Roberts. Second row: 'Curly' Tapp, Baden Hall (behind), Tommy Hayes, Joe Barby, Bert Robinson (behind), Jack Roberts, Tom O'Brien, Mr Toombs, Albert Easteal, Mickey McGlinchey, Ron Bunker (half hidden). Ladies, standing: Edna Hayes, Delia Hall, Rene O'Brien, Mrs Toombs, Vera McGlinchey, Mrs Hall. Front: first two ladies, relatives or friends of Violet Easteal from London, Violet Easteal, Ruby Horne, Dot Whitehead, Lou King.

Winners of the Inter-Group Competition Shield are members of Deanshanger Women's Institute, pictured here in the Memorial Hall, *c.* 1960s. Back row, left to right: Lydia Montgomery, Sue Nicholls, Vera Godfrey, Doris Jarratt. Standing, centre row: Molly Green, Bertha Carslake, Ivena Lea, Mary Gould, Elsie Bellamy, Gladys Nicholls, Rose Matthews, Doris Roberts, Edna Tompkins, Ena Stacey, Doll Pratt, Amy Ridgeway, Doll Godfrey. Sitting: Yvonne Brewer, Gladys Dumbleton, Ivy Masters, Olive Smith, Joan Whittemore, Mrs Rupert Roberts (with shield), Winnie Pascoe, Daisy Robinson, Mrs Sharpe, Maggie Wyatt.

A country scene of yesteryear, *c.* 1910. On the binder is Mr Webb of Grange Farm, Puxley. His son, Alf, is riding the horse, whilst Albert Tapp of Potterspury is standing in front of it. The gentleman in the straw boater is a retired police constable and his son is standing behind him.

The sole reminders of Puxley Wood today are a large decayed oak and its adjacent offspring by the side of the narrow lane between Passenham and the hamlet of Puxley. Known as the King's Standing Oak, it was under this tree, or an ancester of it, that Henry III took up his stand during a hunt while the game was driven past, out of the coverts. (Photograph by Mitch Hicks.)

A typical scene of a flooded Passenham Lane. This lane was often impassable until a few years ago when the River Authority installed an electrical water-monitoring system, so that when the River Ouse rises to a certain level, flooding is avoided.

Coming from the bakehouse in Cross Tree Road, Wicken in about 1931 with Sunday lunches cooked in the bread ovens for a number of villagers. From left to right: Edgar Shakeshaft, Mary Berrill, Ronnie Taylor (carrying tray), Hannah Dawkins (wearing white pinafore), Mrs Chexfield (carrying tray), York Cooper (wearing trilby), Derek Taylor (small boy), -?-, Bert Wrighton (in doorway).

Cake and Ale Ceremony, Wicken, 1964. The Revd Paul Hoskin stands in the centre with church wardens Bill Case on the left and Derek Smith on the right. The ladies are Gwen Tapp, Mrs Vellacott, Rosemary Marchant, Miss Marchant and Mary Carter. This ceremony still continues on Ascension Day with a service commemorating the joining of the parishes of Wyke Hamon and Wyke Dyke in 1587. Worshippers then walk across the Warren to the Gospel Elm where the 'Old Hundredth' is sung. Cake and ale is then served in the village hall. The huge cake is made by Haseldine Bakers in Stony Stratford.

Wicken Cricket Team in about 1946/9. Back row, left to right: W. Harding (umpire), William Ward (supporter), Dave Clark (guest), Tom Arnold (guest), Frank Green, Harold Birdsay, Ray Stokes. Front: Chris Ayres, Norman Ayres, Bill Case, Ron Bunker, A. Dytham (guest), Jim Ward.

Wearing her cross-over apron and her hat, as was her custom in good weather, Mrs Edith Wrighton always did her washing-up under her open porch by her back door. She lived at the Bakehouse, Wicken and is pictured here in the late 1930s.

Drinking outside the Shoulder of Mutton Inn, Calverton, are two regulars with the publican, Harry Holman and his family. He also ran a butchery business; notice the cart on the right hand side of the photo. Left to right: Harry Holman, Lucy, Ethel, Fred, Charlie, Mary, Mrs Ellen Holman, Bill and May.

Obviously a hot day as Mrs Fountaine from Manor Farm is using her umbrella as a parasol! Mrs Penelope Winterbottom is opening a fête in the grounds of Calverton Rectory in the 1940s. The others from the left are Mrs Ravenscroft, Revd R.B. Ravenscroft and Mr Winterbottom.

Oyez! Oyez! decorated a poster advertising an evening with 'goode Squire Ripple to celebrate ye merrie tyme of Chrystmasse, with hys guestes, in ye olden fashione. To include a righte goodlie compainye of Carollers, ye Mummers will acte ye olde Folks Play, "St George", and Roger Merriman will be Lord of Misrule. Ye goode Squire and hys guests will dance ye Minuet, and all ye compainye will dance "Sir Roger de Coverley". Ye merrie Foresters, Olde Father Chrystmasse, Tom Tucker with hys fiddle will join ye revels. Look out for ye Boar's Head, Wassail Bowle, Mince Pies and Yule Cakes and beware of ye Mistletoe Bough. All ye goode people who come to ye revels must pay ONE SHILLING, or better seats kept for ye, paye 1/6 or 2/6.' The proceeds from this entertainment went towards the Northampton General Hospital War Memorial Appeal. The evening was held on 17 and 19 at Calverton and 21 December at Stony Stratford in the 1940s. The bus left Stratford each evening at 7.40 p.m. Back row, left to right: -?-, Connie Rix, Daphne Eales, -?-, Rubin Underwood, Tom Parks, Mrs Violet Wilkes, Ann Markham, Marjorie Dumbleton, Ernie Whitehead. Second row: Ivy Shilson, -?-, Mrs Ela West, William Eales, Mrs Wildman, Mrs Flora Bodfish, -?-, Joan Hassall, Joyce Wilkes, Mr Beckett, Ken Ward. Third row: John Markham, Trevor Jackman, Tony Beckett, Derek Parks, Bob Downing, Roy Foster, John ?. Sitting: ? West, Jennifer Adams, -?-, -?-, Molly Webb, -?-, Clare Wildman, Nina Eales, Brian Edwards. Front row: ? Parks, Harry Wildman, Judy Webb.

The villagers of Calverton in party mood and awaiting their celebration meal for the Coronation of Queen Elizabeth II on 2 June 1953, sitting on straw bales in a barn at Mr Fountaine's Manor Farm. Back row, left to right: Hazel Wilkes, Jane Roberts, -?-, Jane Webb, Les Smith, Mr Lewis, Peter Taylor, Martyn Maycock, John Webb, Michael Webb, Eric West, Ken Weatherhead. Front row: Eileen Roberts, Mrs Lewis, -?-, Jennifer Lewis, Hugh Smith, Mrs Smith, Richard Fountaine, Elizabeth Fountaine, -?-, -?-, John Welch, -?-, -?-, -?-, David Weatherhead, Will West, -?-, -?-.

Sarah Maria Tompkins (Tomkins) of Calverton, born in October 1811, married George Willett of Shenley in 1826. They set sail from Cork on 17 April 1844 on the ship *St Vincent* arriving in Australia on 31 July 1844. They made their way to the Richmond River area where George worked until about 1850, then moved to the Warwick area, working for Leslie Bros on Glengallan ('The Finest Homestead in Queensland') before buying their own farm. They had seven children, George II taking over his father's farm. Sarah Maria was a noted midwife and attended many births in the pioneer years. She died in January 1902 in Warwick, Queensland aged ninety years.

A loaf of bread, 5 ft by 3 ft 6 in and weighing over 100 lbs, formed the centrepiece of the harvest display at Fegan's Homes' Calverton Mission Hall. Made by Wilkie Phelps, baker, 119 High Street, at the bottom it reads 'FEED MY FLOCK' – 1931 – Ezekiel Ch. 34, v. 15. The huge loaf was used to feed the boys on the following Monday. The chapel where the loaf was displayed has now been converted into garages.

Thatching a straw rick at Nash, in the 1940s. To the left is Arthur Colton and W. King; on top of the rick is G. King.

Nash School, c. 1905. Left: Miss Clowes (governess); right: Miss Hillier. Back row, left to right: Arthur Varney, Harry Cowley, Raymond Hogg, Elizabeth Hogg, Mavis Smith, Stella Hogg. Second row: Annie Illing, Coral Varney, Annie Smith, Dorothy Varney, Fred Cowley, George Varney. Third row: Arthur Smith, Norman Varney, Frank Weatherhead, Bill Weatherhead, Walter Hogg, Ivy Hogg. Front row: Wilfred Varney, Nancy Varney, Minnie Illing, Ivy, Ben and Ted Weatherhead.

A popular way to go on a day's outing in August 1906. This group are ready to set off for Bedford from Whaddon with the Band of Hope. The postcard is sent from Tom and Lucy Hopkins to Lucy's sister 'in service' at High Wycombe. Their son, Tom, is sitting at the front left in the waggon.

A sight no longer seen in this area. In this photo, Whaddon Chase Hunt hold their meet at Nash in the late 1960s. The land covered by this hunt has been swallowed up by the city of Milton Keynes which forced them to hunt with, and in the area of, the Bicester & Warden Hill Hunt. The white house in the distance is Weir Cottage.   (Photograph by Ron Summers.)

The hounds are not the only dogs to hunt with the Whaddon Chase. Here is the Whaddon Chase terrier on its way to a meet. It had the job of chasing Master Reynard from his earth.

Pupils at Whaddon School, 1923. Standing, back, left to right: George Young, Jim Hobbs, Ted Wrighton, -?-. Second row: Hugh Willett, Amy Willett, Ted Hayward, Edmund Bryant (from Shenley Common North), George James, Edgar Faulkner, Pat Hales. Left: Miss Pattison (teacher), Freda Shakeshaft. Right: Miss Curtis (headmistress). Sitting: Edna Powell, Eva Willett, Annie Illing, Eva Peverill, Irene Hobbs, Gertie Morris, Doris Holmes, Eva Dormer. Front row: Jack Peverill, Eric Hall, Reg Faulkner, Bill French, -?-, Bill Tearle, Charlie Justice, John Knight.

These Juniors are enjoying taking part in the Whaddon School Summer Play *The Twenty Thieves* in 1967. Back row, left to right: Trevor Formella, Christopher Starr, Peter Dickens, Gillian Illing, Trudy Jaworska, Joy Faulkner, Julie Haywood, Ian McGuinness. On chairs: Amanda Cox, Sandra Collington, Dawn Adams, Helen Jaworska. Front row: Lesley Adams, Dawn Adams, Shiree McGuinness.

Whaddon C of E School pictured on 23 May 1957 with headmistress Miss Dorothy Meadows from Stony Stratford, who was at the school from 1953 until she retired in 1973. She previously worked in Africa for the UMCA (Universities Mission to Central Africa) where she was the village school supervisor. Back row, left to right: Miss Dorothy Meadows (headmistress), Christopher Hammond, -?-, Frederick Hayward, Michael Hammond, Robert Justice, Shirley Ross, Bernard Howell, Richard Formella, Graham Jordan, Linda Beale, Catherine Tombs, Mrs Joan Cross (teacher). Second row: Jackie Fisher, -?-, William Turner, Alan Justice, Keith Robinson, Peter Higgs, Peter Nicholson, George Barnes, Patrick Nicholson, Arthur Johnston, Robert Taylor. Sitting: Kathleen Knight, Valerie Collington, Hilary Cross, Nora Ross, Pat Wrighton, Avril Adams, Susan Malinowski, Antoinette ?, Sheila Illing. Front row: ? Hammond, John Beale, Robert Barnes, Alan Lee, -?-, David Driver, Barry Roff, Peter Bullock.

Resplendent in his postman's uniform, even using a walking stick, is Whaddon's postman, Mr Mackerness, known as 'Old Mac'. He lived in the middle house in Pink's End – now Vicarage Road – and died in the almshouse in about 1935.

After a hard day's work what better than a pint of beer and a game of dominoes with a few mates. In the Lowndes Arms, Whaddon are, left to right: Bill West, George Jones, Stan Turner and Arthur Bowden.

Whaddon Cricket Club in the 1920s. Back row, left to right: Fred Powell, Leslie Smith, Fred Dormer, George Turner, Alf Missenden. Front row: Bert Willett, Mr Taylor, Eric Hall (scorer), George James, Mr Billie King (umpire).

A load of faggots just collected by George Willett of Whaddon, pictured in a country lane near Tattenhoe, c. 1920. He is wearing leather leggings and boots. When the leggings wore out, he cut them up for the soles and heels on children's shoes. The faggots were cut from hazelnut when coppicing and used for bean sticks, pea sticks and hedge binders.

Whaddon Cricket Club Annual Dinner, 1950. Back, top table: Bill Taylor. Back row, left to right: George King, Jeff Hodgkinson, Joyce Hodgkinson, Ted Roff, Fred Hayward, Mrs Fred Hayward, Mrs Hayward snr, Miss Nellie Parrott, Bill Tyrell, Ted Wrighton, Ethel Wrighton, Les Smith, PC Kimber. Row with back to camera: Martin Campbell, Marianna Campbell, Mrs Gray, Mr Gray, Bill Hopkins, Hugh Willett, Gordon Parrott, Leslie Tofield, John Hopkins, Bob West, Norman Bull. Front, left to right: Sam Drayton, Arthur Pettitt, Alf Knight, Alf Marks.

Lacemakers at Shenley Brook End, *c.* 1903. Left to right: Mrs G. Payne, Mary 'Polly' Harris, Clara Willett (with bobbin winder), Hannah Willett, Louisa Kimbel. Tom Harris is holding a book – he used to read to them while they were making their pillowlace.

This pillow-fighting contest at Shenley brought out all the villagers to watch at the celebrations for the Coronation of George V in 1910. The men are smartly dressed in jackets and caps for the fight!

The farmer's wife. Mrs John Hooton fetches water from the well in the yard of Emerson Farm, Shenley Brook End, *c*. 1931.

Delivering milk on Leys Road, Loughton with Jingles the pony is Land Girl Ivy Higgs wearing her Land Army overcoat. She worked for Frank Ebbs of Manor Farm, Shenley Church End in the 1940s.

Shenley's own milk and egg retailer, Mr Henry Jenkins, measuring milk out of his churn for Mrs Neal in Shenley Church End. In August 1932 he was tragically killed on the main Watling Street by a disabled Willys-Knight 6-wheeler 50 cwt lorry, when the chain by which it was being towed, broke. Mr Jenkins was hit while delivering eggs to Brick Kiln Cottages, one mile south of Stony Stratford.

The family from Shenley post office, Mr Henry Shouler and his wife Minnie (née Franklin) with daughters Gertrude and Annie pictured on 17 August 1899. Mr Shouler took over from a family named Nichols in 1895. Gertrude gained the title of postmistress in 1918 on the death of her mother, relinquishing the post in 1948 when she in turn was succeeded by Annie's son, Maurice Goodway and his wife Daphne. When they retired in 1988, after a further forty years and one month of service, the post office which had been in the same family for 100 years closed. The name will now no doubt be perpetuated as it is known as Post Office Corner.

Captured on a *carte-de-visite* is Miss Susan 'Suie' Willett of Shenley on a Sunday afternoon stroll with her young man, *c*. 1895. She was an excellent dressmaker, working for a number of noted families in the area including 'Mrs Dr Bull' of Stony Stratford. No doubt she made the charming costume she is wearing.

Shenley County Primary School, 1956. Back row, left to right: Mr L. Fell (headmaster), Linda Bass, David Chapman, Gillian Parker, Jimmy Swansbury, Ian Collier, Martin Foster, Wendy Chapman, Barry Willett, Barry Davies, Roy Goodway, Billy Shouler, Gerald Collins, Susanne Dolling, Margeurite Pattenden, Hayden Smith, Mrs Steel (teacher), Mrs Priscilla Cox (teacher). Second row: Christine Doddington, Barbara Robinson, Brian Massey, Robin Walduck, Janet File, Jennifer Sykes, Alec Johnson, Denise Groom, Maureen Haddon, Shirley Berry, -?-, Marlene Love, John Grace, Ann Carter, Rosemary Andrews, Karen Haddon, Rosalyn Smith, Edith Radband, Sheila Wright. Third row: Andrew Grey, David Wallace, Janice Robinson, Margaret Dundas, -?-, Keith Moseley, Christina Moseley, John Pattenden, Rosalind Knight, Judith Ebbs, Ann Gascoigne, Eileen Wright, Arthur Radband, Kevin Bodley, Tony Hill, Christine Vine, Jean Barclay, Marilyn McGill, Dennis Ball, Karen Higgs. Front row: Christine Bass, -?-, Steven Ball, -?-, Judith Daniels, -?-, Janet Houghton, -?-, Keith Radband, Keith Owen, Jennifer Collier, Graham Jordan, Marilyn Price, Timothy Price, Marilyn Doddington, -?-, Patrick Goodway, Vernon Pattenden.

(*Opposite, bottom*) Shenley British Legion Party, Women's Section in February 1952. Far table from back: Gladys Bass, Dorothy Markham, Alice Collier, Wyn Dolling, Annie Goodway, Sybil Groom, Mrs Perry, Mrs Hurst, Margaret Collins. Nearside of far table: Mrs Vine, Mrs Moseley, Mrs Higgs, Enid Higgs, Olive Dundas, Jessie Dundas, Mrs Walduck, Mrs Jordan. Front table, clockwise from left: Mrs Morgan, -?-, Joan Parker, Peggy Bodley, Jean Ebbs, Bessie Shouler, Vera Chapman, Daphne Andrews, Ann Bodley, Brenda Ebbs, Margeurite Payne. At back, including: Mrs Sid Willett, Daphne Goodway, Pear Higgs, Marjorie Smith, Joan Durrant, Nora Davis, Mrs Kirby.

The lady who never left school! Born in 1891, Priscilla 'Prissie' Daniels, later Mrs Albert Cox, was one day a pupil at Shenley School and next day a pupil teacher. She continued to teach infants in the same classroom until her retirement in about 1958, some fifty years later. She is pictured here with her class in about 1956. Standing at back, left to right: Philip Smith, Timmy Daniels, Archie Dundas, Gordon Dundas, Caroline Smith, Thelma Stephenson, Remeny Hill, Christina Dolega. Left side of table, front to back: John Wootton, Billy Owen, Richard Bass, Teddy Swainsbury, Christopher Dolega, Terry Hawes. Right side: Roger Willett, Angela Bodley, Paul Balaam, Carol Herety, Bobby Woulds, Susan Foxley.

Pupils of Shenley Church End School, 1932. Their teacher is Mrs Stevens. Back row, left to right: -?-, Henry Hurst, Daisy Masters, Peggy Bodley, Maurice Goodway, Monica Wells, Les Walton. Middle row: Olive Willett, Norma Grosvenor, Erica Markham, Nesta Power, Ivy Perry, Molly Bodley. Front row: -?-, Graham Grosvenor, Cyril Daniels, Don Foxley, Bruce Kimble.

The Holy Thorn is a unique possession of Shenley Village. According to legend, Joseph of Aramathea planted his staff in the ground at Glastonbury, and it grew into a hawthorn bush. Perhaps a pilgrim planted a cutting on the side of the old road from Shenley Church End to Shenley Brook End. This white May blooms at Christmastide, and once again in the summer.

Shenley British Legion, Men's Branch Annual Dinner in an annexe of the Fountain Inn, *c.* 1951. Round the table, clockwise, from left: Henry Jordan, Bill Harris, Reg Cooper, -?-, Cliff Benmore, -?-, -?-, Teddy Shouler, Ken Ebbs, George Higgs, Ted Higgs, Maurice Goodway (behind), Peter Grace, -?-, Bert Weatherly, Don Dundas, Albert Bass, Ron Payne, Bill Reeves.

The Diamond wedding anniversary of Mr and Mrs George King, Shenley in 1930. From left to right: Louie Ebbs, Mrs A. Harris, Mr George King, Mrs Maggie Daniels (behind), Mrs George King, -?- behind, Mrs George Willett, -?- behind.

Fountain Inn, Loughton, photographed when Mr William Bodley was the owner. He was educated at Bedford School and arrived at Loughton in the mid-nineteenth century with his wife Kate, four daughters and two sons, David and Fred.

In 1911 it is recorded that Mr Fred Bodley, born 1857, was another member of the Bodley family to own the Fountain Inn. He was reputed, by all who knew him, to have a great sense of humour. When he died in about 1919 the inn was tenanted and stayed in the Bodley family until the 1930s, when it was sold to a family named Plumb.

This charming thatched cottage was the home of Mrs Charlotte Gregory, a noted pillowlace-maker who is standing in the doorway with relations in the early 1900s. Positioned in Pitcher Lane, Loughton, it has now been demolished and the area is a small car park.

Sitting on his new motorcycle is Edmund ('Ted') Gurney of Loughton. His suit, hat, goggles and gloves would have been very expensive for the period. This model is a Sun, first registered by the Buckinghamshire Motor Vehicle Licensing Department at Aylesbury, almost certainly in 1910; unfortunately the records are missing. The machine was manufactured by the Sun Cycle & Fittings Co. Ltd of Aston Brook Street, Birmingham, which was owned by the Parks family from 1906 until 1960. It is fitted with a proprietary engine of approximately 200 cc – a part not manufactured by Sun.

Shenley and Loughton Football Club, winners of the North Bucks Shield, *c.* 1950. Back row, left to right: Reg Cox (trainer), Bill Willett, Maurice Goodway, Ray MacPhearson, Tom Markham (goalie), Dennis Willett, Nigel Rodway, Mr Harry Hands (president). Front: Ken MacPhearson, Aubrey Childs, Les Parker, Norman Chapman (with shield), ? Bates, Alfie Goodger, Harry Young. This photograph was taken outside the Talbot Public House.

A ring of children singing around the Christmas tree at the Baptist church, Loughton, before presents were distributed in about 1952/3. Clockwise from the girl on left: Irene Stevens, Roger Harper, Catherine Ebbs, Mrs Collier, -?-, Sidney Pateman, Dorothy Wells, Pauline Pateman, Robert Vine, Judith Ebbs, Alec Johnson, Ann Gascoigne, Anne Carter, Christine Vine.

When few cars were seen in Leys Road, Loughton, Mrs Gertie Stevens, a schoolteacher at Shenley, was known to walk down the centre of the road reading her *Daily Mirror*. This picture was taken before the stream was diverted and the road widened.

A sale of work at the Baptist church, Loughton, in the late 1950s. Back left: Ann Bates, Janet Bates, Valerie Willett. Back right: Henry Owen, Dennis Owen, Bruce Garratt. From left: Mrs Bates, Pauline Pateman, Gwen Carter, Mrs Ern Willett, Elsie Cox, Mrs Weatherly, Mrs Amy Gurney, Mrs Marshall, Ethel Foxley, Flo Wells. In front: Tony Hill, Anne Carter. Seated right: Mrs Brett.

Hannah Bird, busy knocking down the old malt house to make way for her garage in the 1970s. The tower of All Saints' Church, Loughton, can be seen in the background.

A smart-looking baker's boy, E.J. Willett (Ern) who worked for S.A. Kitchener & Sons, Loughton, c. 1920. They were selling a 2 lb loaf for 3½d and a 1 lb loaf for 1¾d. On Saturday mornings, extra bread was made, twelve or eighteen 2 lb loaves for charity which were paid for by the Parish Council. It was left in the porch of Shenley Church for the widows and those in need to collect. This practice was discontinued in the 1950s.

The Norman motte and bailey at Old Bradwell was later named the Castle Mound. Here the villagers are square dancing behind the village hall, *c.* 1953.

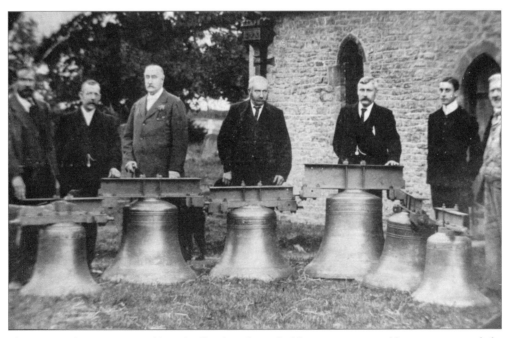

The ringers of St Lawrence, Old Bradwell, when the peal of four was augmented by two more, made by A. Bowell of Ipswich in 1909. Left to right: Charlie Bird, Tom Walters, Revd K.C. Bailey, Tommy Cook, George Walters, Arthur Wootton and Zach Walters.

Friends and members of the Welcome Club, Old Bradwell celebrate the Diamond wedding of Mr and Mrs Harry Stephenson on 1 April 1978. Front row, left to right: Mrs Cross, Mrs Smith, Mrs Wootton, Mrs Harry Stephenson, Mr Harry Stephenson, Mr Barnet. Semicircle from left: Mr Cyril Eakins, Mrs Ellen Eakins, -?-, Mrs Winterburn, -?-, ? Smith, Mrs Grace (Shenley), Mrs Atkins, Mrs Frost, Mrs Whitehead (behind), Mrs Townsend, Mrs Goodger, Mrs Hancock, Mrs Harris, Mrs Smith, Mrs Smith, Mrs Brown, Mrs Atkinson. Back group: Mr Pateman, Mr Cowley (New Bradwell), -?-, Mr Wootton, Mr C. Dickens, Mr Walker (behind), -?-, Mrs Walker, -?- behind, -?-, -?- behind, -?-, -?- behind, -?-, -?- behind, Mrs Dington, Mr Atkinson, -?-, Mr Smith, -?-. Top back: Mrs and Mr Cross.

The youngest radio ham in the country was
Andrew Bellchambers aged fourteen. In 1962
he had to pass a written examination in London
for Amateur Radio. He was given the Call Sign
G3SCF and was a member of North Bucks
Amateur Radio Club.

Old Bradwell Cricket Team in the late 1920s. Back row, left to right: Mr Kirk, C. East, Frank Chapman,
G. East, S. Brown, E. Clarke, W. Kirk, Alec Coley. Front row: Charlie Spiers, G. French, M. Chapman,
G. Brown, E. Walker.

The last service at St Peter's Church was held on the Feast of St Peter, Saturday 29 June 1963 at Stanton Low. Thirty people made a pilgrimage along the canal towpath and across the field to the roofless, derelict and isolated church. Revd R.G.M. Russell, the sixtieth vicar of Stantonbury ended Mass by reciting the last Gospel in Latin, perhaps the same words as used at the first Mass here 750 years ago. Front, left to right: Anthony Cave (server), Martin Chapman, Revd R.G.M. Russell (celebrant), Derek Savage, Percy Cave. Left to right: Mr Franklin, Roy Franklin, Mr West, Mrs Craddock, Frank Mellor. Behind: Mrs Derricutt, Beryl Glenfield, Mrs Bowman, Olive Savage, Mrs Todd, Edith Foddy, Sheena French.

Pictured in the vehicle he used for visiting his patients, Dr Charles Henry Miles of The Laurels, Stantonbury, is seen here at a hospital fête in about 1925 with the Young Imperialists (IMPS) of Wolverton – the forerunners of the Young Conservatives. Born at Fenny Stratford on 8 January 1859, and educated at Trinity College, Old Stratford, he won many prizes including the Government Award twelve times for skilful and efficient vaccination.

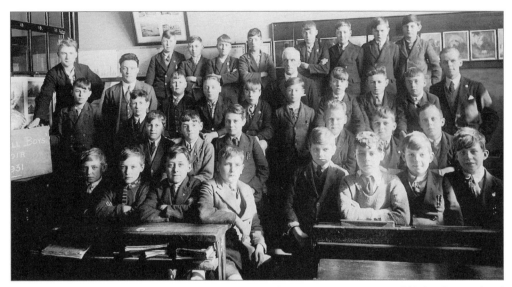

Bradwell Boys School Choir, 1931. In this year they won at the Northampton Eisteddfod and were placed second in Birmingham. Back row, left to right: I. Andrews, Frank Sims, R. Lines, A. Emerton, E. Boughton, S. Baker, Clifford Campbell, W. Teagle. All standing: Sid Roddis, C. Parker, B. Salmons (choirmaster), R. Mynard, George Warner, Dennis Boon, D. Phillips, I. Waite, Irvine Brooks (headmaster), behind, Frank Stonton, E. Sykes, Bill Preston, Mr Kersley (teacher). Seated: Ron McLeod, Jack Henshaw, Ron Green, S. Tapp, Harold Bates, E. Henson. Front row: Doug Labrum, Ray Whewell, Fred Baxter, Doug Lambert, Ray Bellchambers, Eric Batterson, Ken Verrall, Ron Bennett.

Bradwell Boys School, 1949. The teachers and kitchen staff. Back row, left to right: Dai Rees, Bill Coxhill, Ken Healey, Ken Hooton, A. Colby, Jack Gibson. Front row: Mrs Clarke, Miss Cook, Mrs Cosby (cook), Ben Salmon (headmaster), Mrs Smith, Mrs Rose, Mrs Johnson.

Found behind a tapestry sent to be reframed was this old school photograph of a class at St James Church School, Stantonbury, 1900. The boys and their masters are, from the back, left to right: F. Walden, W. Cobley, F. Willis, E. Hale, O. Willis and A. Rigby. Second row: T. Walton, C. Martin, H. Coxhill, E. Hooper, A. Atkins, A. Hyde, G. Powell, F. Kirby, G. Pedder. Third row: S. West, G. Green, M. Bellchambers, R. Stimson, F. Boughton, T. North, J. Parsons, A. Inwood, T. Grant. Fourth row: B. Brewer, O. Mills, Revd A. James (vicar), T.W. Arkwright, T. Arkwright (superintendent), J. Fincher, A. Smith, H. Shackleford. Front row: H. Barnes, E. West, H. Ashley, E. Puryer, H. Nichols, R. Brassett.

(Opposite, bottom) Stantonbury St Peters AFC were founded in 1902. During the 1937/8 season they were winners of the Wolverton Hospital Cup and semifinalists in the Bucks & Berks Junior Cup. Back row, left to right: B. Brazier (committee), W. Hedge, J. Fisher (captain), H. Wyatt, A. Atkinson (trainer). Second row: W. Hyde (committee), W. West (treasurer), T. Monk (committee), C. Scott (auditor), F. Mills, F. Key, R. Dormer, H. Bates, E. Glenn (committee), C. Bissill (committee), W. Wood (committee), F. Chapman (committee), C. Lister. Front row: P. Gaskin (secretary), J. Bates, B. Cook, J. Preston, F. Simms, W. Overton, G. Kirk (chairman).

New Bradwell County Girls School, Standard Seven, *c.* 1932. Back row, left to right: Enid French, Gladys Scott, Ida Nicholls, Winifred Markham, Mabel Stephenson, Mary Turner. Centre: Hilda Nash, Vera Godfrey, -?-, ? Nash, -?-, Vera Owen, May Jones, Winnie Walker. Front row: Florence Odell, Hilda Knight, Winnie Pollard, Elsie Cowley, Joy Gardner.

The Child family of Oak Cottage, Queen Anne Street, New Bradwell in 1902. Standing, left to right: Adelaide, Harry, Arthur, Lilley. Centre row: Elsie, Joseph Child (a signwriter who painted coats of arms on railway coaches in Wolverton), his wife Caroline (née Bradshaw of Lidlington), Ada. Front row: Bertha, Gertrude and Daisy. Adelaide, Arthur and Lilley continued to live in New Bradwell. Ada married Frank Stanton who ran the Stanton Bakery on the eastern corner of Queen Anne Street and Newport Road.

Long Service employees from the Wolverton Carriage & Wagon Works, Stores Office, c. 1953. Of all the girls working in this office, the three in the photo had the longest service. Back row, left to right: Arthur Ostler, Bert Frere, Bill Riddy, Rene Fox, Arthur May, Harold Swannell, Percy Lloyd, Horace Hill. Front row: Bill Brown, Clifford Howarth, Mary Francis, Sid Bourner, George Jackson, Arthur (Jack) Webb, Olive Webb, Ben Phillips, Arthur Barby.

Shown here wearing their Sunday best of pin stripes, cravats and a variety of hats are the first men of the Joiners Shop of the L&NWR Carriage & Wagon Works, Wolverton, in 1884, following the change from a Locomotive Works. Back row, left to right: E. Newman, J. Haynes, G.H. Snowdon, S. Harvey, W. Gazeley, T. Cherry, J. Millward, G. Berridge. Front row: J. Joyce, J. Hewlett, W. Belton, J. Knight (foreman), T.H. Ward, G. Gibbs, A. Pinfold (Method Study).

The Brass Shop Athletic Team won 'The Works' (Railway Carriage & Wagon Works) Inter-Shop Competition at Whitsun Sports in Wolverton Park, *c.* 1950. Back row, left to right: P. Hillyer, P. Hands, T. Smith, J. Mynard, C. Healey, M. Riley. Front row: J. Tofield, E. Sutton.

The Works annual holiday! Employees and their families from the Carriage & Wagon Works wait on Wolverton Station in 1976. In 1938 5,000 people worked there and special trains were run: three to Blackpool, one to North Wales, one to Yarmouth and one to London. In group, left to right: Mr Parker, behind, Phil Daniels, Mrs Alderman, Bill Ley, behind, Roy Alderman, Bernard Cross, Sandra Cross, Ted Whitehead, Mrs Whitehead, Mrs Cross, Miss Cross, Frank Atkins, Mrs Folwell, Tom Folwell. Children, front: Stephen Cross, Linda Alderman.

One of the annual Christmas parties of McCorquodale & Co. Ltd, Envelope Makers & Printers in Wolverton, c. 1954/6. Mr William Rowledge was MC (Master of Ceremonies), for a number of years. Top table, left to right: Anne Rowledge, Mrs Louie Rowledge, Bill Rowledge, A. Kirby, Mrs Kirby, Mr Herbert E. Meacham, Mrs Enid Meacham, Kenneth Carter, Mrs Carter. Left front: -?-, Bernard Bryan, Barry Bryan, -?-, -?-, -?-, -?-, -?-. Right front: Jean Davies, -?-, -?-, -?-, -?-, -?-, -?-, Charlie Walding, Mrs Walding.

Wolverton Cycling Club, *c.* 1885. This gathering mostly consists of penny-farthing bicycles which were invented in 1871 by James Starley. These were very dangerous machines as the rider was at least 8 feet from the ground. Paragon Cycles advertised these models from £3 3*s* 8*d*. Dr Miles of Bradwell is riding an early tricycle known as a Coventry Rotary, invented in 1885. A variation of the penny-farthing, it had a chain drive to the large wheel and was steered with the small wheels.

Post Office Tellers of the Government stationers, McCorquodale & Co. Ltd, *c.* 1952. Top row, left to right: Mr Beech, Beryl Phillips, Margaret Barden, Molly Adams, Peggy Archer. Second row: Mary Hickson, Yvonne Bird, Edna Hurst, Cynthia Clark. Third row: Winnie Hudson, Renie Kendal, Iris Howe, Iris Harris, Mrs MacTavish, Jean Twigg. Fourth row: Daphne McLeod, Sid Rowledge, Mr Yates, Miss Tompkins, Joy Evans, Beryl Bruce. Front row: Valerie Mead, Mrs Grace, Phyllis Tyson, Margaret Bird, Sylvia Kay.

Wolverton Town Football Club, founded 1887. This photograph shows the 1st Team winners of the Buckingham Hospital Cup and South Midlands League in 1938/9, pictured on the lawn of Craufurd Arms Hotel. Back row, left to right: Reg Brown, Cliff Harding, Doug Frost. Centre row: Fred Atterbury, Charlie Lawman, Cyril Evans, Wally Cook (goalie), Sid Tubbs, Johnny Cooper, Fred Sayers, ? Radcliffe. Front row: Arthur Russell, George Dicks, George Eales, Charlie Morley, Jack Smith.

Wolverton Town Football Club in a training session, c. 1948. Left to right: -?-, -?-, Peter Hillyer, -?-, -?-, Dai Owens, Jack Goldsmith, Dick Riley (captain), -?-, -?-, Ken Dormer, Tommy Parks.

Dancing to Joe Lovesey's Old Tyme Orchestra, probably in the Wolverton Railway Works Canteen. A musician for forty-seven years, Joe formed his own ten to twelve piece orchestra in 1946, playing in halls throughout four counties and in London for twenty years.

Members of the Wolverton Urban District Council in 1948/9. The Council had twenty-one members, Messrs Tom Haseldine, Kitchen and McLeod are absent from this picture. The WUDC ended its fifty-five year reign on 1 April 1974. In its place came the Milton Keynes Borough Council. Back row, left to right: Dr Eric Fildes, W. Jim Geen, Dr Delahunty, Owen Sabin. Centre row: Harry Wildman, Dr J. Love, Col. Hagley, Bert Timms, Len Squires, Herbert Lunn. Front row: Miss Aileen Button, Tom Parker, H.E. Meacham, OBE, Mr Jeffrey (Clerk to the Council), Stanley Woollard, William H. Lee, George Clark, Donald E. Morgan, Mr T.J. Tibbetts.

Swimming at the Wolverton Public Bathing Place, in the River Ouse, sometime during the years preceeding the opening of the Wolverton Swimming Pool in 1964. This section of river was to be found below the railway viaduct, along the Haversham Road.

BICU (Bucks Club & Institute Union) Juvenile Angling Contest in the 1950s, competing just behind the Railway Works. Presenting the trophies was Bert Turvey of Bradwell, a keen angler. BICU had the fishing rights from Black Horse Inn to Galleon Inn Bridge on the Grand Union Canal. The contest was revived in 1951 after a lapse of ten years. Back row, left to right: Alan Campbell, Bob Gregory, Ro Cook, Roy Campbell, Ray Styles, -?-, Pat Dearn. Half-hidden row: Geoffrey Odell, -?-, -?-, Christopher Bear, Terry Valentine, Brian Clark, Archie Scragg, Roy Clutton, -?-. Third row: Bert Turvey, Derek Stones, Barry Rowledge (receiving cups), -?-, ? Bear, ? Hancock, ? Campbell, Dave Griffith, ? Berridge. Front row: ? Lovell, Ivor Price, Roger Ellis, Freddie Buckingham, -?-, -?-.

Wolverton Girls School, Market Hall, Creed Street, Wolverton – now the Madcap Theatre. Starting as a railway school, built and opened in 1840, these premises were kept for girls and infants when a mixed school opened in Church Street in 1896. The Creed Street School closed in 1907 when the new Elementary School in Aylesbury Street was completed in 1906. The class pictured is Standard II. Back row, second from left: Dora Power. Second row from back, fourth from right: Florence Price, whose family originated from Tingewick.

Wolverton Boys School Choir pictured in St George's Vicarage garden. They were the winners of the Northampton and District Challenge Shield in 1930. Back row, left to right: Mr H. Lunn (headmaster & choirmaster), Macdonald Walters, Douglas Norman, Cliff Meakins, T. Murphy, Cyril Carvell, Vic Espley, Cliff Marshall, Ron Howe, Jack Mills, R. Burrows. Second row: Len Little, Charlie Stephens, Eric Castle, Allan Morrall, Stan Clarke, Eddie Hart. Third row: Reg Mead, Arthur King, Ron White, John Smith, Alec Russell, Peter Howell, ? Clarke, Len Nicholls. Front row: Les Wilson, George Johnson, Bill Coxhill, Percy Lowe, Fred Frisby, Tom Sear.

Mr H. Lunn (Bert) was headmaster of Wolverton Boys School from 1926 to 1947 and was reappointed headmaster when the school became a co-educational secondary modern school in 1947. He was a very strict disciplinarian in every aspect of education and apart from his many outside school activities – councillor, freemason, bowls player and keen supporter of Yorkshire County Cricket XI – he was also a very keen musician and singer. He was choirmaster of St Mary's Church and St George's Church, Wolverton, but his pride and joy was the formation of his school choir from 1927 onwards.

The Boys' Choir received great accolades from all the musical festivals they entered and had many successes; year after year in Buckingham, Bedford, Berkhamsted, Birmingham, Northampton, Kettering and Central Hall, Westminster. They won the LMS Challenge Cup at the Temperance Union Festival on no fewer than eight out of ten occasions and as recognition of these successes, the cup was given to the school. Armstrong Gibbs, reputed to be the greatest living judge of children's choirs, gave to Mr Lunn's choir the highest marks, 98 out of 100, that he had ever given to a choir. The possessor of a fine tenor voice, Mr Lunn was a gold medalist himself and in 1935 he won the challenge rose bowl at Northampton Musical Festival.

Wolverton Infants School, Aylesbury Street, *c.* 1933. Back row, left to right: Peter Held, Joyce Harrison, Jim Dewick, Kath Cook, Arthur Hurst, Avery Longmore, Eric Rice, Marjorie Welford, Bobby Gowland. Centre row: -?-, Cyril Tompkins, Muriel Castle, Cecil Johnstone, Marjorie Bedson, Bob Percival, Joan Beeton, Bob Griffiths, Marie Elliott, Maurice Wills. Sitting: Joan Coxhill, Stanley Smith, Beryl Cobley, Ken Tagg, Sylvia Long, Derek Dormer, Joan Chambers, Mavis Underwood, Joan Bush. Front row: Peggy Yates, Joan Lee, Enid Bubb.

The two projectionists at the Empire Cinema, Church Street, Wolverton are Tony Mills and John Tompkins. Their Monarc projector is in the foreground. In approximately 1926 this building was gutted, completely redecorated and opened as a cinema. It closed down when the lease ran out on 17 May 1969; the last films shown here were *Carry on Screaming* and *Carry on Cleo*.

The well-known firm of Franklin's, builders of Stony Stratford, are seen building Nos 82 & 80 and 78 & 76 Victoria Street, Wolverton, *c.* 1900. George Franklin, the founder of the firm, could build these high chimneys 'by eye' and without the aid of a spirit-level. At back, left: George Franklin and son Ted Franklin. Standing, front left: son John Franklin, Sam Tarry, -?-. Front: Two tradesmen carpenters, names unknown.

Outside their home at 21 Young Street, Wolverton, are Peter (left), Pauline and Raymond Briggs, *c.* 1930. This was a typical house of those built by the L&NWR Company in the 1830s. The Council, having bought the 'Little Streets' – Creed Street, Ledsam Street, Young Street and Glyn Square – for £18,000, demolished them in the early 1960s.

1st Wolverton Boy Scouts, formed on 23 February 1908, is the fifth oldest group in the country still in existence and the oldest in the county of Buckinghamshire. The photo shows the group in 1948. Back row, left to right: Francis Craddock, John Wallace, Ronald West, Royston Stanton, Barry Styles, William Dempster, Derrick Keeves, Brian Stimpson, Ron Hockley, Michael Dormer, Milford Callow, Gerald Goodridge. Second row: Michael Woodward, John Clarke, John Kingston, Gerald Johnson, Fredrick Warner, David Cook, Lawrence Dowdy, Colin West, Robert Smith, Peter Haynes, Royston Johnson, Peter Hempstead. Third row: Mr William Henson, Brian Taylor, John Timms, Richard Ratcliffe, John Stevens, Colin Broom, Keith Webb, John Hawtin, Peter Taylor, John Rainbow, Ken Ruffhead, Gerald Hooton, Michael Lovesy, Mr Harold Clarke. Fourth row: Mr William Eady, Mrs Enid Coxhill, Mrs Perrin, Mary Jakeman, Bill Coxhill, George Cook, Dick Saunders (District Commissioner), Mr Walter J. Parker, Ken Clarke, Eileen Jakeman, Mr Walter Clarke, Mr William Winsor, Mr William Brown. Front row: Roy Scrivener, Ronnie Parrot, -?-, Frank Jones, Michael Kingston, Mike Mellor, Brian Wise, Alan Herring, Peter Rainbow, Derrick Stones, Barry Bryan, Bernard Bryan.

1st Wolverton Girl Guides were the first Guide company to be formed in the Wolverton District in 1919 by Miss Sylvia Harnett of Wolverton Vicarage, later Commissioner Harnett. This group are pictured in 1948. Back row, left to right: Betty Kightley, Eileen Bandy, Thelma Robinson, Joan Robinson, Molly Carroll, Ruth Denton, Margaret Thomson, Molly Dunkley, Yvonne Carroll. Centre: Brenda Clark, Margaret Taylor, Rita Gregory, Marjorie Hart, Mary Jakeman (Lieutenant), Miss Beatrice Fairs (District Commissioner), Mary Lidster (captain), Enid Whitlock, Evelyn Horlock, Anita Clarke. Front row: Ann Adams, Eileen Gawkrodger, Jill Clamp, Prudence Brown, Janet Snow, Janet Lovesy, May Henson.

The official photographer for the local newspaper *Wolverton Express*, Tom Brown, is seen here capturing Bob Swann's wedding on film at Wolverton in the 1950s. He was a full-time professional photographer and operated from his home in Windsor Street.

Monday was wash day in the 1930s. Mrs Minnie Eakins is hanging out her washing at her home in Jersey Road, Wolverton. She is wearing a coarse apron which she also wore when digging the garden. The wooden line-prop was a type sold by hawkers and wicker baskets were in common use.

A Wolverton entry in their carnival, 'A Puppet Makers Workshop', in the 1970s. Left to right: Mrs Susan Garwood, Joanne Mayo, Gail Battrum, Mrs Glad Mayo, Kay Roberts, Andrew Mayo, Denise Blackwell, Vivian Sanderson, -?-, -?-, Patrick Atter, Mrs Win Blackwell, Christopher Jones, Kay Holbrook.

A street party in Anson Road, Wolverton after the proclamation by Winston Churchill that 8 May 1945 was VE Day. Round the table from left corner round to right corner: Jill Richardson, Madeline Jones, Marie Onan, Mavis Peer, Margaret Thomson, -?-, -?-, -?-, -?-, -?-, -?-, Harold Greenwood, Ivor Brown, Graham Garrett, ? Holman. Behind children from left to right: Vic Peer, Joe Little, Mrs Greenwood, Mrs Richardson, Mrs Peer, Mrs Pam Jones, -?-, Kathleen Little, Mrs Long, Mrs Cox, -?-, Frank Garratt, -?-, Mrs Garratt, -?-, -?-, Mrs Gillard, Hazel Holman, Mr Holman. Around back from left: -?-, Mrs Brown, -?-, Mrs Ellis, Fred Perkins, Mrs Thompson, Mrs Brown, -?-, -?-, Mr Harry Cooper, Mrs Dorothy Cooper, Eileen Hobson, Myrtle Long, -?-, Mr Alf Thompson, -?-. Right-hand side from back: Miss Doll Swain, Mr Fred Sutton, -?- Mr Long, -?-, Miss Kate Shirley, -?-, Mr George Shirley, Mr Greenwood. The house on the left is 72 Anson Road, the Cooper family home: Aylesbury Street runs horizontally across the street towards the top of the picture and in the distance in Stratford Road is McCorquodale's Works.

Wolverton Home Guard during the Second World War. Back row, left to right: Arnold Birkett, Ralph Williams, Tom Jones, George Cave, Jack Griffiths, Cecil Webber, Percy W. Roberts, George Clark. Front row: Herbert Severn, ? Coleman, Sid Dytham, Tom Hopcroft, officer in charge (name unknown), Frank Mayo, Henry Cooper, George Wyatt.

Pupils of Miss Catt's Dancing School which was held on Saturday mornings in the ballroom of the Victoria Hotel, Wolverton. In this dancing display, *c*. 1930, the elves include John Habgood, second from right, while first on the left is his sister Pamela.

A favourite spot for the children from Clarence Road, Stony Stratford to go swimming; in the River Ouse, near Maycock's Mill, Old Wolverton in the 1940s. Back row, left to right: Alan Goodridge, David Nash, John Aylott, Joy Aylott, Roy Skipper, Leslie Shean, Madeline Townsend, Brian Townsend, John Osborne, David Osborne, Brian Tompkins, Sheila Lake, Norman Webster. Front row: Janet Skipper, Maureen Wildman, Alan Peat, Geoffrey Pallett, Pat Rolfe, Ken Shean.

Standing on the bridge over the River Ouse at Old Wolverton Mill are Audrey and Eileen Waine in their York House School uniforms, c. 1938.   (Photograph, Mrs Herbert Waine.)

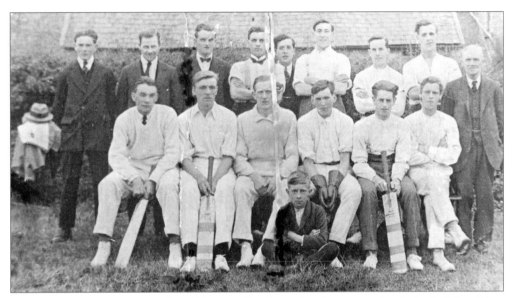

Holy Trinity Old Wolverton Cricket Club pictured in front of the barn situated at the back of Slated Row houses in the Galleon Inn field. They were winners of the North Bucks League in 1921. Mr Reg Westley has the medal won by his father, Gilbert Westley. Back row, left to right: Arthur Bowdler, -?-, -?-, -?-, Arthur Morris, Reg Eales, -?-, Tom Haycock, old Mr Bowdler. Sitting: -?-, Gilbert Westley, Rupert Meadows, -?-, Arthur Lamb, Sid Neale. Front row: George Eales (ball boy). Who is skulking behind the newspaper?

The firm of S. Holland & Sons transporting Territorials to Wolverton station en route to a camp before the First World War. Harry Cooper is fifth from the left. The driver (right) is Samuel Holland's youngest son, Stafford, accompanied by his mate, his cousin Bertie Holland who was nicknamed Chummy. The engine is a Tasker 5-ton Compound 'Little Giant' tractor, works number 1399, which was new to Samuel Holland in 1909 and registered AA2293 in Hampshire where Tasker's works was situated.

ACKNOWLEDGEMENTS

I would firstly like to thank my husband, Jim Lambert, for his considerable assistance with the preparation of this book by providing transport for the 400 miles covered, for showing his extensive knowledge of places, past residents and events in the area and for checking my typewritten captions.

I am also greatly indebted to Lord Habgood for agreeing to write the foreword to a book covering an area with which he was once so familiar.

Some photographs could not have been included without the assistance of Ray Rowlson Photographers and Roger Welling who restored and copied old photographs. Also, thanks to Ron Unwin for copies from the Wolverton and District Archaeological Society's slide collection.

A special mention must go to Richard Odell for allowing access to his father, Ron Odell's postcard collection; Bill West, a local author, for use of his material; Don Hellings and Gerald Ditum for their help in using the Hanslope & District Historical Society archives; the Milton Keynes Museum of Industry and Rural Life for research and to Robert Ayers, Ron Hockley, Larry Francis, Bob and Tony Wain, Bill Coxhill, Ray Bellchambers, Reg Westley, Keith Henson, Evelyn Jaworska and Doug Holloway for their historical details and local knowledge.

Thanks are also due to the many people who have given their time and hospitality and willingly loaned their family photographs, scrapbooks and books of reference: Frank Atkins, Joan Atkins, Connie Beadman, Mary Bellchambers, Bill Bessell, Hannah Bird, Peggy Bodley, Peter Briggs, Joan Brockway, Dorothea Burgess, Canon C.H.J. Cavell-Northam, Dorothy & Denis Chipperfield, Ruth Clare, Ken Clarke, Nancy Colborne, John Cooper, Arthur Cowley, Brenda Cox, Enid Coxhill, Beryl Croxford, George Dicks, Ken Dillow, Muriel Ditum, Joan Dolling, Dorothy Ebbs, Barbara Flack, Olive Foxley, Julie Franklin, Sylvia and Gerald Freestone, Kathleen Gardner, Eva Gascoigne, Jack and Alan Goodridge, Daphne & Maurice Goodway, Mitch Hicks, Peter Hillyer, Ken Holbrook, Irene Holland, Betty Holloway, Phyllis and John Holman, Malcolm Hooton, George Horton, Roy Keeves, Margaret Ladd, Olive and Ted Lambert, Betty Lane, Ivena Lea, Phyllis and Les Lovesy, Peggy and Bob Martin, Dorothy Meadows, Phyllis Leete (SS Methodist Church), Nola Mikkelsen (Australia), Tony Monk, Kay Moroney, David Nash, Ralph Nichols, Arthur Noble, Marjorie Norman, Jose Oakley, Rosalie and John Osborne, Revd Ian Phelps, Doreen Phillpotts, Louie Rowledge, Mary Saggers, Syd Sharp, Ken Shean, Lesley Shean, Sylvia Sibthorp, Ann Stainsby, Jean Starsmore, Gweneth Stock, Margaret and Ron Summers, Kitty Tite, Sylvia Tombs, Jean Tweedale, Daphne Tween, Hazel Wallis, Marion Watts, Evelyn Webb, George Webb, Trevor Wells, Bob West, Ann Westley, Maurice Weston, Olive Wickson, Janet Williams, Keith Wilyman; Alex Wootton, David Yates. If I have inadvertently omitted anyone from the above list, I trust they will accept my sincere apologies.

Equally valuable has been the help of a number of people who identified faces in group photographs, thus providing as complete a record as possible.

BRITAIN IN OLD PHOTOGRAPHS

To order any of these titles please telephone our distributor, Littlehampton Book Services on 01903 721596
For a catalogue of these and our other titles please ring Regina Schinner on 01453 731114